dBASE II™

USER'S

GUIDE

Adam B. Green

Revised and Updated

SoftwareBanc

A Spectrum Book

Prentice-Hall, Inc., Englewood Cliffs, New Jersey 07632

i

Library of Congress Cataloging in Publication Data

Green, Adam.
     dBASE II User's Guide

     "A Spectrum Book."
     1. dBASE II -- Instruction. I. Title
ISBN 0-13-196519-0

This book is available at a special discount when ordered in bulk quantities. Contact Prentice-Hall, Inc., General Publishing Division, Special Sales, Englewood Cliffs, N.J. 07632

A SPECTRUM BOOK

10   9   8   7   6   5   4

Printed in the United States of America

ISBN 0-13-196519-0

PRENTICE-HALL INTERNATIONAL, INC., London
PRENTICE-HALL OF AUSTRALIA PTY. LIMITED, Sydney
PRENTICE-HALL CANADA INC., Toronto
PRENTICE-HALL OF INDIA PRIVATE LIMITED, New Dehli
PRENTICE-HALL OF JAPAN, INC., Tokyo
PRENTICE-HALL OF SOUTHEAST ASIA PTE. LTD., Singapore
WHITEHALL BOOKS LIMITED, Wellington, New Zealand
EDITORA PRENTICE-HALL DO BRASIL LTDA., Rio de Janeiro

7057892

iii

TABLE OF CONTENTS

CHAPTER 3   INTRODUCTION TO PROGRAMMING

CHAPTER 4   DEVELOPING STANDARD dBASE II TECHNIQUES

CHAPTER 5   DESIGNING A COMPLETE dBASE II SYSTEM

CHAPTER 1

INTRODUCTION

What is dBASE II?

The best way to understand dBASE II is to think of it as a word processor for data. A word processor allows you to manipulate characters, words, sentences and pages to create a document that fits your needs. dBASE II allows you to work with fields, records, and files to manage your data in just the way you want.

Word processing is responsible for placing microcomputers in offices around the world. For many people, it is an easy concept to understand, and the resulting increase in office productivity quickly justifies the original purchase of a computer system.

Once people become comfortable with storing documents and assorted information in their computer, they soon feel the need to maintain their records in a more orderly fashion. The logical step is to seek out a means of doing data processing.

To make this as simple as possible, while providing the necessary power, dBASE II provides many data management facilities. Among these are an interactive query language, (which means you can "talk" to it), a report writer to create tabular reports, and a powerful programming language allowing a knowledgeable person to adapt dBASE II to the needs of those who are less familiar with computers. Many other features make dBASE II ideally suited to solving business applications.

The author's first experience with dBASE II

I started looking for a product like dBASE II in December, 1980, while working as the product manager for a New England based chain of retail microcomputer stores. Our stores had been selling mostly APPLE II computers, and had a need for software which would run on APPLEs and computers which used the CP/M operating system. One type of software product needed was a data base system which could be used by novices as well as more knowledgeable users. Being a methodical person, I started a thorough search of the software market.

Two months, ten sets of manuals and five demo disks later, the desired product still had not been found. Evaluating software can be a frustrating task. Often you don't know exactly what you want until you find it. This was the case with the Great Data Base Search. I wasn't giving up until I found something that got me really excited.

One day in early February, I found an ad in BYTE magazine for dBASE II. Above a picture of the dBASE II manual next to a

bilge pump, was a headline which said, "dBASE II vs. the Bilge
Pumps." The ad went on to say, "We all know that bilge pumps
suck. And by now, we've found out - the hard way - that a lot of
software seems to work the same way." Although the ad may have
been in poor taste, I had to agree with it. The ad included an
offer of a 30-day money back guarantee, which was unique in my
experience. I quickly ordered a copy of dBASE II. After all, how
could I lose?

When dBASE II arrived, I learned how the 30 day guarantee
worked. Included with the manual were two disks. One was a demo
disk which performed all the functions of dBASE II, with a
limitation of fifteen records per data file. The second disk,
sealed in plastic, contained a complete version of the program.
The customer could return the package for a full refund within
thirty days, if the plastic seal was unbroken. Ashton-Tate, the
publisher of dBASE II, claimed that the return rate was less than
three percent.

Within a few hours, I knew dBASE II was what the stores
needed. In fact, it was better than I had thought possible. The
next week was spent madly clicking away at the keyboard, while my
wife made sure I remembered to eat and sleep.

At the same time I was learning dBASE II, I was also in
charge of implementing a computerized inventory system for the
retail stores. I was so sure of what this program could do that I
opened my big mouth and said, "Don't worry, dBASE II will allow
me to whip something up in a few weeks." Unfortunately, I was one
of the only programmers around, so everyone believed me.

When programmers give a time estimate, it is wise to raise
it to the next interval of time and multiply by 2. This would
have me finishing in 4 to 5 months.

A few days later, I was told that I would be attending the
West Coast Computer Faire in San Francisco the last week in
March, so I wouldn't be present to help take the end of month
inventory. I had made my foolish claim at the end of February,
which left me less than a month to see that all of the current
data was entered into dBASE II, write a system which would be
powerful enough to handle a full end of month physical inventory,
and was both so simple to operate and free of bugs that it would
work without my being there. Don't laugh, I'm sure most of you
programmers out there have found yourselves in similar
situations.

Luckily, not being the type to panic, I just kissed my wife
goodbye and prepared myself for a month of all-nighters. Things
went well for the first two weeks and it began to look like the
deadline would be reached. I ended up not working all night and
even got to see my wife occasionally. Of course, this was the
perfect time for Murphy's Law to strike.

One day, less than two weeks before I was scheduled to leave for San Francisco, I was called into the president's office and informed that the results of my program would be used by our auditors to determine the value of the company's inventory.

This demonstrates a fundamental principle of data processing, "The more a program is needed, the faster the users become dependent on it. If a program is needed badly enough, the users become dependent on it before it is completed." I just mumbled an incoherent acknowledgment and went back to my terminal.

Less than a week and a half before the deadline, disaster struck as a bug in dBASE II. While it was admittedly a small one, it was sitting right in the middle of my most important program. I frantically called Ashton-Tate and spoke to George Tate, who gave my name and number to the author of dBASE II, Wayne Ratliff. Wayne called later that same day, to tell me that the bug had been found, and that a new disk was on its way.

The disk arrived a few days later, and sure enough the bug was gone. Wayne had also added a few new features from my wish list. This kind of fast response from a software publisher is not typical, believe me.

The program was finished with three days to spare. The rest of the week was spent testing the system and teaching the data entry people how to use it. This proved to be an easy task, as the programs I had written were completely menu driven and had plenty of error trapping.

On my return from a wonderful time at the Faire, I found that only 2 bugs had appeared in my programs. One inventory item had the wrong stock number, and a report had the wrong heading. If I had been programming in BASIC, I would be writing code to this day.

Ever since then, I have been a total dBASE II fanatic. I teach courses on dBASE II, have started a dBASE II users group, and take every chance to talk at computer club meetings about dBASE II. My wife finally gave in and learned dBASE II. Now she has something to talk with me about.

Why was this book written?

This book was written to supplement the manual which accompanies dBASE II, not to replace it. It is hoped that the material covered in this book will provide a basic subset of commands and techniques. You may then read the manual to find a more detailed explanation of all the commands.

CHAPTER 1   INTRODUCTION

dBASE II is a large program with many features available. It is necessary that the manual document every command with all possible variations. This book is not under the same constraints so many commands will be totally ignored. In some cases you will be told to refer to the manual for specific details on keystrokes and syntax. This leaves more space to discuss methods of designing and building dBASE II systems.

How much computer background is assumed?

In a word, the answer is "none." The book will provide as much background material as possible. The approach will be to start off with subjects that assume no background, and build up to more sophisticated examples. Readers at any level of knowledge may work their way up to more advanced topics.

You will find that this "bootstrap" method works well if the examples are followed in order. If you don't get everything on the first reading, the second time around will make it more clear.

It is like reading BYTE magazine. When you first get interested in microcomputers, you can't understand anything in BYTE. With time, you can understand all the ads.

Which version of dBASE II will be discussed?

This book will assume that the reader is currently, or will be, using version 2.3 or greater. Ashton-Tate has guaranteed that all versions after 2.3 will be fully compatible. New editions of this book will be released if any major changes are made to the program. If you own an earlier version than 2.3, you should contact Ashton-Tate for an update.

Which computers are covered by this book?

The dBASE II program is essentially the same on all computers, whether you own an OSBORNE 1 or an IBM Personal Computer. You can write a program in dBASE II on a North Star 8 bit computer, and run it on a Victor 16 bit computer. This makes dBASE II an excellent language for systems developers.

Of course, absolute compatibility is impossible. Since some computers have different operating systems, a few dBASE II commands might not work the same way on all computers. This book will assume that you have the CP/M operating system. Any incompatibility between CP/M and MS-DOS, the other major microcomputer operating system, will be mentioned when necessary.

Who should read this book?

dBASE II is being used by people of various backgrounds. Since this book will build a foundation for any technical material presented, any user of dBASE II will benefit from reading it. The best approach is to start at the first page and keep going until it becomes too technical. People familiar with dBASE II should still read the first few chapters.

CHAPTER 2

dBASE II FUNDAMENTALS

Talking to dBASE II

There are two basic ways of allowing humans to communicate with computers. They are through menus or programming languages. Most commonly used programs are "menu driven", in which a list of options is displayed. A typical example would be an accounting program, which would display the following:

```
--------------------------------------------------------------
                  XYZ   ACCOUNTING SYSTEM

            1.   Accounts Payable

            2.   Accounts Receivable

            3.   General Ledger

            4.   Payroll

        CHOOSE ONE OF THE ABOVE:
--------------------------------------------------------------
```

If the number for the payroll program is chosen, a second menu would allow the selection of various payroll functions. Someone unfamiliar with the program is led through any operation.

The primary disadvantage of this is the time it takes to present the menus and receive the next instruction. Five to six menus may have to be displayed before the desired function is reached. The main menu may then have to be returned to before starting a new operation. Menu driven programs are useful when dealing with first time users, but increased familiarity with the system may create a desire to get the job done more directly.

dBASE II uses the "command driven" approach, in which the task to be performed is described with a special language. These commands have specific meanings, and require strict adherence to a proper syntax. A knowledgeable user may quickly perform any desired task without working through menus.

The obvious catch is the word knowledgeable. People buy a computer so that it may do their work for them. Often they are not prepared to spend time learning how to operate the computer. After all, anyone can watch TV or use a telephone without any practice. Why is it necessary to learn a new language in order to use a computer? Since a computer is a general purpose device which has unlimited potential, new sets of commands must be learned for each different application. dBASE II provides the language to make your computer a data base machine.

Using an inventory application as an example, a list of items which cost more than $1,000 could be obtained with the following commands:

```
USE INVEN
LIST ALL ITEM, VENDOR FOR COST > 1000.00
```

A menu driven program could never give results this easily.

If you feel that learning many commands will take more time than you have, don't worry. There are a few essential commands which will perform most tasks. If the menu approach still seems more comfortable, take heart. A program may be written in the dBASE II language which uses menus, thus offering the best of both worlds. For now, give the command approach a try.

dBASE II syntax

All languages have a set of grammatical rules for constructing sentences. This is called the "syntax" of the language. The syntax of computer languages is usually rigid where punctuation and ordering of commands are involved. Often the correct placement of commas and semicolons takes the longest time to learn. The language should be consistent enough in its syntax rules that users may easily combine commands into new combinations.

When a language is designed for non-programmers, an attempt is usually made to simulate the syntax of English. To speed the learning process, the program should offer explanations when a mistake is made. The error message should be as English-like as possible. Responding to a typing mistake with "SN ERROR" is not helpful.

Most dBASE II commands use the following format:

VERB   SCOPE   NOUN   CONDITION

Verbs describe the action to be performed, and are usually self explanatory. Common verbs are; LIST, USE, and DISPLAY. The scope limits the range of the verb's use. A verb might operate on the entire file or just the next 5 records, in which case, the scopes would be ALL and NEXT 5, respectively. The noun is the object on which the verb acts, and may be a file, field, or variable. The condition selects the nouns to be acted on.

Questions of syntax can get tiresome, so don't be too concerned with grammatical rules. The syntax of dBASE II is just as rigid as most languages, but it is similar enough to English to make learning it a natural growth process. If there is an error, dBASE II will attempt to explain the mistake, and suggest a correction.

Here are some sample commands:

VERB	SCOPE	NOUN	CONDITION
DELETE	ALL		FOR PAYMENT = 0
DISPLAY	NEXT 10	NAME	
LIST		NAME, CITY	FOR CITY = "BOSTON"

As you can see, it is not always necessary to include all of the parts of a dBASE II sentence. Often the scope and noun are implied. A condition is only included if a select group of nouns is to be acted upon by the verb.

Don't try to memorize the commands that are used in the examples. If you just practice with your copy of the program, the rules of syntax will seem natural in time.

Disk files

A disk file is simply a series of characters which the computer has written on the magnetic media of the floppy or hard disk. It is similar to the method used to record sounds on a cassette recorder. The computer can store many thousands of names and addresses, and search through them at a great rate.

The computer's disk storage is used for more than just saving names and addresses. A common series of commands may be saved on a disk file, and used at any time without re-typing. The memory limitations of a microcomputer may be overcome by using the disk as a note pad for temporary or permanent storage. Working through the fundamentals of dBASE II will offer many opportunities to recognize functions using disk storage.

Using examples from sample dBASE II sessions

Let's play a little, and try out some of the basic commands. We will build a small mailing list, and see what can be done with it. Please type these examples into your computer as well, since the commands used here will be needed for future examples.

When dBASE II is ready to receive a command, it will print a period at the beginning of a line. This prompt means that the program is waiting for you. This brevity may be a little disconcerting at first.

The examples in this book are set off from the text by dashes. To help you follow the examples, **BOLD FACE** words are those entered by a human and normal type words are the responses from dBASE II. All commands have been capitalized for clarity, but lower case commands work just as well. dBASE II commands have been capitalized in the text as well as the examples. The symbol for a carriage return in the examples is <CR>.

To simplify the typing required, the first four letters of a command are sufficient for dBASE II. This is similar to a computer game called Adventure. For clarity, all commands in the examples will be typed in full.

Use more than one disk drive

For some computers with smaller floppy disks, such as the APPLE II, it is necessary to place dBASE II on drive A:, and data files on drive B:. dBASE II assumes that all files are on the same disk drive as itself. Files on different drives must be named with the drive letter followed by the file name. For instance, a file called MAIL on drive B: would be called B:MAIL. If most of your files are on a different drive from dBASE II, a new default drive may be specified. This would be done with the command "SET DEFAULT TO B:". dBASE II then assumes that all files are on drive B:, unless a new drive is specified.

CREATE a data file

Before saving information in a file on the disk, a description of the data must be entered. Each field in the new file is given a name, type, and length. Together the fields make up a record, and their format is called the file's STRUCTURE. Every record has the same format, even though each holds different information. A data file is similar to a table of information, where each line is a record and each column is a field.

Each field must have a name of ten characters or less, and it is best to use a name which will give some idea of the contents. All of the fields in MAIL.DBF will contain mixtures of numbers and letters, so their type has been entered as "C", for character. If arithmetic is to be performed on a field, the type must be specified as "N", for numeric. A logical field, one which is either true or false, is defined as type "L".

The size of a field determines the amount of room taken up on the disk. All fields are stored as their full size, and any unused spaces are filled with blanks.

Reserving too much room for a field will quickly waste the disk storage available. On the other hand, leaving too little room will create a problem when Rumplestiltskin asks to be placed on the mailing list. Don't be too concerned, as any field's size may be changed later.

Each record may contain up to 32 fields. Each character field may be up to 254 characters in length, and numeric fields up to 10 digits. Logical fields are always 1 character in length. The total size of all the fields in a record may reach 1000 characters. A maximum of 65,535 records may be stored in any data file.

. CREATE

ENTER FILENAME: **MAIL**

ENTER RECORD STRUCTURE AS FOLLOWS:
```
FIELD    NAME,TYPE,WIDTH,DECIMAL PLACES
001      FIRST,C,10
002      LAST,C,10
003      ADDRESS,C,20
004      CITY,C,10
005      STATE,C,2
006      ZIP,C,5
007      <CR>
```

INPUT DATA NOW? **N**

A file called MAIL.DBF has now been created on the disk. The ending of DBF is added automatically, so that MAIL may be recognized as a data file when a directory of the disk is read. Room has been assigned for first name, last name, address, city, state, and zip code.

USE a data file

In keeping with an English-like style, you select a file to work with by giving the command USE. When the USE command is given, dBASE II stops USEing any previous data file. Once a file is USEd dBASE II will assume that all commands refer to that file. Later on we will see how to USE more than one file at a time.

. USE MAIL

You can now work with the file called MAIL.DBF. In computer terms this would be called "opening" the file. If you are a BASIC programmer, you should be thrilled to know that USE replaces all OPEN and FIELD statements in BASIC. This alone should justify a switch to dBASE II.

APPEND records to a data file

Now that MAIL.DBF has been created, information may be added
to the file with the APPEND command. APPEND lets you move the
cursor to any field, and enter or change the information. When
you are finished with that record, simply move past the last
field. dBASE II will then present a new record. To tell dBASE II
that you don't want to enter any more names, simply press return
on the first field of a new record. The information is then saved
into the disk file being USEd.

. APPEND

```
RECORD 00001
FIRST     : MAX
LAST      : SMITH
ADDRESS   : 100 FEDERAL ST.
CITY      : BOSTON
STATE     : MA
ZIP       : 01284

RECORD 00002
FIRST     : SALLY
LAST      : FIELDS
ADDRESS   : 30 W. ALEMEDA ST.
CITY      : ST. LOUIS
STATE     : MO
ZIP       : 97821

RECORD 00003
FIRST     : JIM
LAST      : JONES
ADDRESS   : 1 CENTER ST.
CITY      : ARLINGTON
STATE     : MA
ZIP       : 02174

RECORD 00004
FIRST     : <CR>
```

When entering information, take advantage of the full screen
editing feature. Pressing special keys moves the cursor from
field to field, allowing previously entered information to be
modified. The appendix of the dBASE II manual lists the keys to
use for this full screen feature. If the cursor keys do not work
correctly, re-read the section in the manual on installation, or
talk to your computer dealer.

LIST a data file's contents

Now that the names are saved on the disk, they may be displayed on the screen with the LIST command.

```
. LIST

00001   MAX        SMITH      100 FEDERAL ST.      BOSTON      MA 01284
00002   SALLY      FIELDS     30 W. ALEMEDA ST.    ST. LOUIS   MO 97821
00003   JIM        JONES      1 CENTER ST.         ARLINGTON   MA 02174

. LIST LAST

00001   SMITH
00002   FIELDS
00003   JONES

. LIST LAST,CITY

00001   SMITH      BOSTON
00002   FIELDS     ST. LOUIS
00003   JONES      ARLINGTON

. LIST FOR CITY = "BOSTON"

00001   MAX        SMITH      100 FEDERAL ST.      BOSTON      MA 01284
```

Looking at a data file is easy. The entire file or selected fields may be LISTed on the screen. If necessary, only the records which meet certain criteria will be LISTed. All that you need to know are the field names.

The number displayed before the data is called the record number, and it is assigned to every record as it is APPENDed. This number will be used to check the physical sequence of the records in the data file.

Use a printer

Anything that appears on the screen can also be sent to a printer by typing a control-p. This involves holding down the key marked "ctrl", while hitting the "p" key. The first control-p tells dBASE II to start sending anything on the screen to the printer, and the second turns it off. Once the printer is on, all dBASE II commands remain unchanged.

SORT a data file

A common need in keeping a mailing list is to print the names in alphabetical order by last name or zip code. This is accomplished by either SORTing or INDEXing the file.

SORTing a file is done by giving the name of the field to SORT by, and the name of a new data file. The original file will be read, and an alphabetized version saved with the new file name.

The name of the new SORTed file should give some indication of its origin, but any name will do.

. LIST LAST,ZIP

```
00001   SMITH        01284
00002   FIELDS       97821
00003   JONES        02174
```

. SORT ON ZIP TO MAILZIP

SORT COMPLETE

. USE MAILZIP

. LIST LAST,ZIP

```
00001   SMITH        01284
00002   JONES        02174
00003   FIELDS       97821
```

A new data file, named MAILZIP.DBF, has been created on the disk. The physical sequence of the records is in zip code order, as can be seen from the record numbers. The original MAIL.DBF is left on the disk as it was. An obvious limitation of SORTing is the space required by the new SORTed file. Also, any new records appended to the end of the SORTed file will not be in SORTed order. The major factor against SORTing a file is the length of time it takes. dBASE II is usually a very fast program, but SORT is the slowest command in the language. It can take up to an hour to SORT 1500 records on a floppy disk.

INDEX a data file

Instead of SORTing a file, an INDEX may be created based on any field. The field used for the INDEX is called the key field. A new file is created which contains one entry for every record in the data file. This entry holds the contents of the key field,

and the corresponding record number. It is similar to the index
of a book, which contains a list of keywords and the pages on
which they may be found.

. USE MAIL

. INDEX ON LAST TO MAILLAST

00003 RECORDS INDEXED

. USE MAIL INDEX MAILLAST

. LIST LAST

00002   FIELDS
00003   JONES
00001   SMITH

     The INDEX file for MAIL.DBF has been saved on the disk as
MAILLAST.NDX, and is based on the field called LAST. INDEX files
are stored in a form that humans can't easily read, but if
translated they would look like the following:

          FIELDS   2
          JONES   3
          SMITH   1

     If a data file is USEd with an associated INDEX file, all
dBASE II commands, such as LIST, will act as if the file is in
INDEX order. The record numbers show that the records are
actually still in the original physical sequence.

     Since INDEXing a file does not require a complete copy to be
made, substantial savings in disk storage are realized when
compared to SORTing. If any additions are made to the file while
the INDEX is in USE,   the INDEX will be updated automatically.
INDEXing is also at least 3 to 4 times faster than SORTing.

     Many indices may be created for a data file, and up to seven
may be USEd at one time. Unfortunately, keeping many indices
updated will decrease the speed of dBASE II. In practice only
three INDEX files should be USEd at once.

     An additional benefit of INDEXing a file, is the ability to
use the FIND command. The contents of the INDEXed field are
given, and dBASE II searches for the matching record. If there is
no match for the search request, an error message will be
displayed on the screen. The FIND command is extremely fast, and
it usually takes less than two seconds to FIND any record.

. FIND JONES

. DISPLAY

00003 JIM   JONES   1 CENTER ST.   ARLINGTON   MA 02174

. FIND FORD

NO FIND

If dBASE II can't FIND the requested key, a message of "NO FIND" will be displayed.

To SORT or to INDEX, that is the question

So far INDEXing seems to be better than SORTing. There are situations in which it might be better to SORT a file. When you need to look at every record in turn, as in printing labels, it is faster to USE a file which has been SORTed into the desired sequence. This is because all of the records are physically in the correct order, while INDEXed files only appear to be in order. dBASE II has to perform fewer disk operations to retrieve the SORTed records. Here are is an example which will show the kind of analysis you should perform.

```
Creating the ordered file :
INDEXing                   5 minutes
SORTing                   20 minutes
                          ==========
Extra time to SORT        15 minutes


Printing labels:
SORTed file                         5 minutes
INDEXed file                       10 minutes
                                   ==========
Extra time to print INDEXed file   5 minutes
```

If this set of labels is printed more than 3 times on the same file, it is faster overall to SORT the file. When all the records in a file are to processed in order several times, a SORTed file is better than an INDEXed file.

DBPlus

Since there are obviously applications which can benefit from SORTed files, dBASE II user's have always needed a faster way to do this. A new product, called DBPlus, has been released by HumanSoft. This program performs several functions on dBASE II files, including SORTing files up to 15 times faster than dBASE II itself. DBPlus can also SORT on all the fields in a file at one time, while dBASE II can only SORT one field at a time. It is also 2 to 3 times faster than dBASE II's INDEX.

Write REPORTs

The LIST command is one way of looking at a data file's contents. When a more formal listing of the contents of a data file is necessary, the REPORT command is available. This command allows the design of a tabular REPORT which is then displayed on the screen, or sent to the printer.

Designing a REPORT is similar to CREATEing a data file. The contents of each column must be described by giving the width and name of the data field to be displayed. Each column may also be given a heading which will be printed at the top of every page. Besides displaying the contents of a pre-existing field, a column may also represent an arithmetic operation on any combination of fields. Thus, if PRICE is a data field, tax may be reported by specifying a column to be equal to PRICE * 0.05.

The REPORT may include totals of numeric fields, and breaks for subtotals when the contents of a specified field changes. This is useful for departmental expense summaries and other financial REPORTs.

A REPORT heading may be specified, and this will be printed at the top of every page along with the date and page number.

```
. USE MAIL

. REPORT FORM MAILLIST
ENTER OPTIONS, M=LEFT MARGIN, L=LINES/PAGE, W=PAGE WIDTH
PAGE HEADING? (Y/N) Y
ENTER PAGE HEADING: MAILING LIST REPORT
DOUBLE SPACE REPORT? (Y/N) N
ARE TOTALS REQUIRED? (Y/N) N
COL      WIDTH,CONTENTS
001      10,FIRST
ENTER HEADING: NAME
002      10,LAST
ENTER HEADING:
003      10,CITY
ENTER HEADING: CITY
004      <CR>
```

This REPORT specification is saved on the disk as MAILLIST.FRM. It may be printed at any time by repeating the REPORT command. If a condition is specified the REPORT will only be printed for those records that match the condition.

. REPORT FORM MAILLIST

        PAGE NO. 00001
        12/1/82

                                        MAILING LIST REPORT

            NAME   CITY

        MAX   SMITH   BOSTON
        SALLY   FIELDS   ST. LOUIS
        JIM   JONES   ARLINGTON

. REPORT FORM MAILLIST FOR CITY = "BOSTON"

        PAGE NO. 00001
        12/1/82

                                        MAILING LIST REPORT

            NAME   CITY

        MAX   SMITH   BOSTON

If it is necessary to modify the report, any word processor may be used to edit MAILLIST.FRM. When done editing the file just save it back to the disk and dBASE II can use it later.

EDIT and REPLACE MISTAKES

An important part of the data entry process is the isolation and correction of errors. After new records are APPENDed, they should be LISTed on the printer and verified. Once a mistake is found, there are several ways to correct it. The simplest of which is the EDIT command. The record number to EDIT must be given at the same time.

Like the APPEND command, EDIT allows full screen operation. This means that the entire record's contents are displayed, and the cursor may be moved to any field. We will now EDIT the second record so that Sally is changed to Sidney. We can tell dBASE II to stop EDITing by pressing control-W.

```
--------------------------------------------------------------
. LIST

00001  MAX        SMITH       100 FEDERAL ST.       BOSTON     MA 01284
00002  SALLY      FIELDS      30 W. ALEMEDA ST.     ST. LOUIS  MO 97821
00003  JIM        JONES       1 CENTER ST.          ARLINGTON  MA 02174

. EDIT 2

RECORD 00002
FIRST      : SIDNEY
LAST       : FIELDS
ADDRESS    : 30 W. ALEMEDA ST.
CITY       : ST. LOUIS
STATE      : MO
ZIP        : 97821

. LIST

00001  MAX        SMITH       100 FEDERAL ST.       BOSTON     MA 01284
00002  SIDNEY     FIELDS      30 W. ALEMEDA ST.     ST. LOUIS  MO 97821
00003  JIM        JONES       1 CENTER ST.          ARLINGTON  MA 02174
--------------------------------------------------------------
```

The EDIT command could put back Sally's name, but a similar command, REPLACE, will be used instead. The record number is typed first, followed by the information to be REPLACEd in the named field. If the scope is defined as ALL, every record will have the change made. Of course dBASE II doesn't warn you if the REPLACE is silly. Since there is no UNREPLACE command you should make a copy of the data file before performing a major REPLACE. This can be done with the dBASE II COPY command.

```
--------------------------------------------------------------
. 2

. REPLACE FIRST WITH "SALLY"

00001 REPLACEMENT(S)

. DISPLAY

00002  SALLY      FIELDS      30 W. ALEMEDA ST.     ST. LOUIS  MO 97821

. COPY TO TEST

. USE TEST

. REPLACE ALL FIRST WITH "MAX"

00003 REPLACEMENT(S)
```

. LIST

```
00001   MAX          SMITH        100 FEDERAL ST.      BOSTON       MA 01284
00002   MAX          FIELDS       30 W. ALEMEDA ST.    ST. LOUIS    MO 97821
00003   MAX          JONES        1 CENTER ST.         ARLINGTON    MA 02174
```

That was a trivial example of the REPLACE command. Its true power is shown in a hypothetical inventory application.

USE INV-FILE
REPLACE ALL COST WITH COST * 1.10

The cost of all our hypothetical stock items have just been increased by 10%. How's that for inflation?

DELETE records from a data file

Most data base programs make removing a record a difficult process. This is why a check for $0.00 is often impossible to remove from a computerized billing system. With dBASE II, it is no problem. Just enter the record number to work with, followed by the DELETE command.

. USE MAIL

. LIST

```
00001   MAX          SMITH        100 FEDERAL ST.      BOSTON       MA 01284
00002   SALLY        FIELDS       30 W. ALEMEDA ST.    ST. LOUIS    MO 97821
00003   JIM          JONES        1 CENTER ST.         ARLINGTON    MA 02174
```

. 1

. DELETE

00001 DELETION(S)

. DISPLAY

```
00001 *MAX          SMITH        100 FEDERAL ST.      BOSTON       MA 01284
```

The record is still in the file, and has been marked with an asterisk for deletion later. dBASE II follows the safe method of removing records. They are first marked with the DELETE command, and then removed with the PACK command. This way you have a chance to change your mind and RECALL the record before PACKing it. PACK is permanent so you might want to make a copy of your old file before PACKing it. This gives you a backup for safety.

```
----------------------------------------------------------------

. RECALL

00001 RECALL(S)

. DISPLAY

00001  MAX         SMITH        100 FEDERAL ST.        BOSTON        MA 01284

. COPY TO TEST2

. USE TEST2

. 1

. DELETE

00001 DELETION(S)

. PACK

PACK COMPLETE, 00002 RECORDS COPIED

. LIST

00001  SALLY       FIELDS       30 W. ALEMEDA ST.      ST. LOUIS   MO 97821
00002  JIM         JONES        1 CENTER ST.           ARLINGTON   MA 02174
----------------------------------------------------------------
```

The new file, TEST2.DBF, now contains only 2 records. As you can see the record numbers have been adjusted. The old data is still in MAIL.DBF, and we will continue to use that for our examples.

Use dBASE II's memory

Besides storing information on the disk, you may also store often used facts in the computer's memory. This will be very important when you start programming. Sixty four storage places are set aside for memory variables, and these variables may each hold up to 254 characters, a 10 digit number, or the value of TRUE or FALSE.

It is not necessary to tell dBASE II the size and type of a memory variable, as it will be deduced from the contents. Information is saved in a memory variable with the STORE command. All memory variables may be LISTed at any time with the command LIST MEMORY.

```
------------------------------------------------------------
. STORE "FRED"  TO NAME

FRED

. LIST MEMORY

NAME          (C)  FRED
** TOTAL **       01 VARIABLES USED  00004 BYTES USED

. STORE 100 TO AMOUNT

100

. LIST MEMORY

NAME          (C)  FRED
AMOUNT        (N)   100
** TOTAL **       02 VARIABLES USED  00010 BYTES USED
------------------------------------------------------------
```

The contents of a particular memory variable may be displayed with the ? command. This can be translated as "what is" or "print."

```
------------------------------------------------------------
. ? NAME

FRED

. ? 10 * AMOUNT

1000
------------------------------------------------------------
```

All of the memory variables may be saved in a disk file with the SAVE TO command. This creates a file with the ending of MEM. The variables are brought back into memory with the RESTORE FROM command. If you want to remove a variable you just RELEASE it.

```
------------------------------------------------------------
. LIST MEMORY

NAME          (C)  FRED
AMOUNT        (N)   100
** TOTAL **       02 VARIABLES USED  00010 BYTES USED

. SAVE TO TEST

. RELEASE NAME
```

```
. LIST MEMORY

AMOUNT        (N)    100
** TOTAL **        01 VARIABLES USED  00006 BYTES USED


. RELEASE ALL

. LIST MEMORY

** TOTAL **        00 VARIABLES USED  00000 BYTES USED

. RESTORE FROM TEST

. LIST MEMORY

NAME          (C)   FRED
AMOUNT        (N)   100
** TOTAL **        02 VARIABLES USED  00010 BYTES USED
```

     The   file created in the previous example was called
TEST.MEM, and is completely different from TEST.DBF created
earlier.

Record pointer

     When USEing a data file, dBASE II is always keeping track of
the current record being worked on. To accomplish this, the
current record number is saved under the name # in the memory of
the computer. This memory variable is known as the record
pointer. A pointer is a number which refers to a location. Just
as your zip code refers to your house's location, the record
pointer refers to the current record.

     To find the current record number, we ask for the value of
the record pointer. To look at the current record we say DISPLAY.
When we first USE a file, the first record is the current record.
This is called TOP by dBASE II. The last record is called BOTTOM.
To move to the next record we SKIP. Entering a record number will
make that the new current record.

```
. USE MAIL

. GOTO TOP

. ? #

1
```

. DISPLAY

00001 MAX   SMITH   100 FEDERAL ST.   BOSTON   MA 01284

. SKIP

RECORD: 00002

. DISPLAY

00002 SALLY   FIELDS   30 W. ALEMEDA ST.   ST. LOUIS   MO 97821

. 1

. DISPLAY

00001 MAX   SMITH   100 FEDERAL ST.   BOSTON   MA 01284

       If an INDEX is USEd, the record pointer works in INDEX
order. When the FIND command is used, dBASE II stores the record
number found in the record pointer. If the record can't be found,
dBASE II stores 0 in the record pointer.

. USE MAIL INDEX MAILLAST

. FIND JONES

. ? #

3

. DISPLAY

00003 JIM   JONES   1 CENTER ST.   ARLINGTON   MA 02174

. FIND FORD

NO FIND

. ? #

0

. GOTO TOP

. DISPLAY

00002 SALLY   FIELDS   30 W. ALEMEDA ST.   ST. LOUIS   MO 97821

The record pointer should always be considered when performing any function. When a function's effect on the record pointer is understood, the full power of the function is realized.

System variables

The record pointer is an example of a system variable. These are memory variables maintained automatically by dBASE II.

Two useful system variables are DATE() and EOF. The date is recorded in memory when dBASE II asks for it at the start of the program. EOF stands for the end of the data file and will be used in programs to make sure the last record has been reached. When the record pointer is positioned past the last record, EOF is stored as true.

```
. ? DATE()

12/1/82

. GOTO BOTTOM

. SKIP

. ? EOF

.T.
```

USE more than one data file

dBASE II reserves two areas of memory for data files. So far we have been working in the PRIMARY area of memory. This is where dBASE II starts. If we need to USE another data file at the same time, we must SELECT SECONDARY. This will open the other area of memory. A USE command in the SECONDARY area will not affect a file in USE in PRIMARY. SELECT PRIMARY moves us back to the PRIMARY area.

```
. SELECT PRIMARY

. USE MAIL

. LIST

00001  MAX      SMITH     100 FEDERAL ST.       BOSTON      MA 01284
00002  SALLY    FIELDS    30 W. ALEMEDA ST.     ST. LOUIS   MO 97821
00003  JIM      JONES     1 CENTER ST.          ARLINGTON   MA 02174
```

. SELECT SECONDARY

. USE MAILZIP

. LIST LAST

```
00001   SMITH
00002   JONES
00003   FIELDS
```

. SELECT PRIMARY

Both MAIL.DBF and MAILZIP.DBF are now being USEd at the same time.

Macros

It is often necessary to type the same command repeatedly. The typing chore can be lessened by STOREing the command into a memory variable. This variable can then used in place of the longer command. If an & is placed in front of a variable name, dBASE II will act as if the contents of the variable were typed. This use of a memory variable to replace an entire command is called a MACRO.

Programmers often use macros to write a shorthand language.

.USE MAIL

. STORE "LIST" TO L

LIST

. &L

```
00001   MAX     SMITH    100 FEDERAL ST.     BOSTON     MA 01284
00002   SALLY   FIELDS   30 W. ALEMEDA ST.   ST. LOUIS  MO 97821
00003   JIM     JONES    1 CENTER ST.        ARLINGTON  MA 02174
```

Internal STRUCTURE of a data file

The names, types, and sizes of the fields make up the file's STRUCTURE. This information is stored at the front of every data file in a block of characters called the file header. DBASE II can determine the STRUCTURE of any data file in USE by reading this header. The command LIST STRUCTURE displays this information.

. **LIST STRUCTURE**

```
STRUCTURE FOR FILE:   MAIL.DBF
NUMBER OF RECORDS:    00003
DATE OF LAST UPDATE: 12/1/82
PRIMARY USE DATABASE
FLD        NAME      TYPE WIDTH     DEC
001        FIRST      C    010
002        LAST       C    010
003        ADDRESS    C    020
004        CITY       C    010
005        STATE      C    002
006        ZIP        C    005
** TOTAL **                00058
```

Besides storing information about the file's STRUCTURE, the header also holds the number of records in the file, and the date when the file was last added to or modified.

The **STRUCTURE** of **MAIL.DBF** tells us that each record takes up 58 characters on the disk. Once the total number of records to be placed in a file is known, the required storage space may be calculated. This is equal to the number of records multiplied by the length of each record. An additional 512 characters must be added for the header.

By looking at the STRUCTURE of a file, anyone will know how to access a data file created by others. Many people and programs may thus share the same data files easily.

MODIFY the STRUCTURE of a data file

One factor to count on in any computer application is change. A common saying in the computer field is that "any program which is running is obsolete."

There are several reasons for this inevitable change. The users will rarely have a good understanding of their existing manual systems, which makes implementing a computerized system difficult. Secondly, the introduction of any computer system will cause the users to change their view of the computer's capability. One common request is, "if it can do that, can't it also do this one little extra function." These little extras can keep a project going forever.

To keep up with changing data base needs, it is necessary to have an understanding of the techniques involved in changing the STRUCTURE of a data file. We will examine some of these techniques.

Every method of changing the STRUCTURE of a data file involves the creation of a new data file with the desired STRUCTURE and data. The old file is always left as a backup assuring the safety of any data entered.

If the CREATE command is used to define the new data file, a variation of the familiar APPEND command may be used. The new data file is USEd, and data is APPENDed FROM the old file.

dBASE II will read the headers of each file and look for fields with matching names in each file. It will then transfer data, between matching fields only, one record at a time.

Let's change the STRUCTURE of MAIL.DBF with this method, removing the city field, adding a phone number field, and shortening the last name field.

. CREATE

ENTER FILENAME: NEWMAIL
ENTER RECORD STRUCTURE AS FOLLOWS:
  FIELD   NAME,TYPE,WIDTH,DECIMAL PLACES
  001   FIRST,C,10
  002   LAST,C,4
  003   ADDRESS,C,20
  004   STATE,C,2
  005   ZIP,C,5
  006   PHONE,C,13
  007   <CR>

INPUT DATA NOW? N

. USE NEWMAIL

. APPEND FROM MAIL

00003 RECORDS ADDED

. LIST

```
00001  MAX        SMIT 100 FEDERAL ST.      MA 01284
00002  SALLY      FIEL 30 W. ALEMEDA ST.    MO 97821
00003  JIM        JONE 1 CENTER ST.         MA 02174
```

The new file NEWMAIL.DBF now has the desired STRUCTURE, and the data was transferred to the appropriate fields automatically. Fields missing from the old file were ignored, matching fields were given as much information as they could hold, and new fields were left empty. The new empty field, PHONE, can be filled in manually with the EDIT or REPLACE commands.

A method which requires less typing involves the use of the
COPY command. If a subset of an existing file is needed, the old
file is USEd and selected fields COPYed to a new file.

. USE MAIL

. COPY FIELD FIRST,LAST,STATE TO NEWMAIL2

00003 RECORDS COPIED

. USE NEWMAIL2

. LIST STRUCTURE

STRUCTURE FOR FILE: NEWMAIL2.DBF
NUMBER OF RECORDS: 00003
DATE OF LAST UPDATE: 12/1/82
PRIMARY USE DATABASE

FLD	NAME	TYPE	WIDTH	DEC
001	FIRST	C	010	
002	LAST	C	010	
003	STATE	C	002	
** TOTAL **			00023	

. LIST

00001	MAX	SMITH	MA
00002	SALLY	FIELDS	MO
00003	JIM	JONES	MA

    If more extensive changes are necessary, only the STRUCTURE
may be COPYed to the new file. This new file may then be USEd,
and the STRUCTURE MODIFYed. MODIFY STRUCTURE will destroy any
data in the file, which is why an empty version of the original
file must be created first. After the structure is MODIFYed, the
data is APPENDed FROM the old file. Since the MODIFY STRUCTURE
command involves full screen editing of the file header, we will
only see the result in the example below.

. USE MAIL

. COPY STRUCTURE TO NEWMAIL3

. USE NEWMAIL3

. LIST STRUCTURE

```
STRUCTURE FOR FILE:  NEWMAIL3.DBF
NUMBER OF RECORDS:   00000
DATE OF LAST UPDATE: 12/1/82
PRIMARY USE DATABASE
FLD        NAME       TYPE WIDTH    DEC
001     FIRST         C     010
002     LAST          C     010
003     ADDRESS       C     020
004     CITY          C     010
005     STATE         C     002
006     ZIP           C     005
** TOTAL **                 00058
```

. MODIFY STRUCTURE

MODIFY ERASES ALL DATA RECORDS ... PROCEED? (Y/N) Y

. LIST STRUCTURE

```
STRUCTURE FOR FILE:  NEWMAIL3.DBF
NUMBER OF RECORDS:   00000
DATE OF LAST UPDATE: 12/1/82
PRIMARY USE DATABASE
FLD        NAME       TYPE WIDTH    DEC
001     FIRST         C     010
002     ADDRESS       C     020
003     CITY          C     010
004     ZIP           C     005
005     STATE         C     002
** TOTAL **                 00048
```

. APPEND FROM MAIL

00003 RECORDS ADDED

. LIST

```
00001   MAX       100 FEDERAL ST.     BOSTON      01284 MA
00002   SALLY     30 W. ALEMEDA ST.   ST. LOUIS   97821 MO
00003   JIM       1 CENTER ST.        ARLINGTON   02174 MA
-----------------------------------------------------------------
```

The names of existing fields have always been kept constant.
In that way, dBASE II was able to tell which fields were to be
transferred. A more complex procedure is necessary to change the
names of fields.

The old data file must be COPYed to the disk without the
header. When the data is APPENDed into the new file, the relative
positions instead of the field names will be used to place the
data in the new fields.

. USE MAIL

. COPY TO MAILTEMP SDF

00003 RECORDS COPIED

     A file named MAILTEMP.TXT has now been created on the disk.
The SDF command specified that the data would be saved without a
header. This is how it looks:

```
MAX        SMITH      100 FEDERAL ST.     BOSTON      MA01284
SALLY      FIELDS     30 W. ALEMEDA ST.   ST. LOUIS   MO97821
JIM        JONES      1 CENTER ST.        ARLINGTON   MA02174
```

. COPY STRUCTURE TO NEWMAIL4

. USE NEWMAIL4

. MODIFY STRUCTURE

MODIFY ERASES ALL DATA RECORDS ... PROCEED? (Y/N) Y

. LIST STRUCTURE

```
STRUCTURE FOR FILE:  NEWMAIL4.DBF
NUMBER OF RECORDS:   00000
DATE OF LAST UPDATE: 12/1/82
PRIMARY USE DATABASE
FLD        NAME      TYPE WIDTH     DEC
001        FIRST:NAME  C     010
002        LAST:NAME   C     010
003        ADDR        C     020
004        CITY        C     010
005        STATE       C     002
006        ZIP         C     005
** TOTAL **                 00058
```

. APPEND FROM MAILTEMP SDF

00003 RECORDS ADDED

. LIST

```
00001  MAX        SMITH      100 FEDERAL ST.     BOSTON      MA 01284
00002  SALLY      FIELDS     30 W. ALEMEDA ST.   ST. LOUIS   MO 97821
00003  JIM        JONES      1 CENTER ST.        ARLINGTON   MA 02174
```

Another type of file change would be the creation of a file which has the same STRUCTURE, but only contains selected records. This is simplest of all, and only requires a condition to be specified for the APPEND FROM or COPY TO commands.

. USE MAIL

. COPY STRUCTURE TO NEWMAIL5

. USE NEWMAIL5

. APPEND FROM MAIL FOR CITY = "BOSTON"

00001 RECORDS ADDED

. LIST

00001 MAX   SMITH   100 FEDERAL ST.   BOSTON   MA 01284

. USE MAIL

. COPY TO NEWMAIL6 FOR CITY = "BOSTON"

00001 RECORDS COPIED

. USE NEWMAIL6

. LIST

00001 MAX   SMITH   100 FEDERAL ST.   BOSTON   MA 01284

All of these techniques have their use, and the choice is a matter of personal taste. The important thing is to get a feel for the ways to move data around from file to file.

QUIT a dBASE II session

Now that we have finished our little sample dBASE II session, the logical thing is to stop the program. NEVER end a session by pressing the reset button, or turning the computer off. This might result in loss of recently added data, or damage to existing data files. The only proper method is to say QUIT.

. QUIT

*** END RUN   dBASE II   ***

Conclusion

By now you are either excited by the incredible potential
open to you, or else you are wondering if the 30 day limit has
expired on your guarantee. To the first group, welcome to the
wonderful world of dBASE II. The others shouldn't give up before
reading the manual and the rest of this book. With a little
practice you will be CREATEing, APPENDing and MODIFYing like a
pro.

CHAPTER 3

INTRODUCTION TO PROGRAMMING

CHAPTER 3   INTRODUCTION TO PROGRAMMING

Why write dBASE II programs?

So far we have been typing out each command, when we wanted dBASE II to perform a series of functions. Once a routine is established, users will begin to repeat sets of commands frequently. When that happens, the natural desire would be to simply enter a brief command and have dBASE II repeat the entire procedure for us.

In a sense, new commands would be added to the dBASE II language. Right now dBASE II will take care of all the work involved in handling a disk file, when we say USE. Wouldn't it be nice if we could have labels printed just as easily by saying LABELS? After this chapter you will be doing just that.

The commands we have been using with dBASE II function identically from within a program. This makes it easy to test out an idea interactively before actually writing the program, speeding development greatly.

Who should learn how to program in dBASE II?

People with widely varying computer backgrounds are now using dBASE II. Some users have been programming in COBOL for 15 years, while others have their first exposure to programming when they buy dBASE II. Others will never need to write any programs, but will benefit from an overview of the dBASE II language.

While managers may be the experts on the requirements of an application, a lack of knowledge about dBASE II may interfere with their ability to explain the fine points to a programmer. Reading this chapter will make them better able to understand the potentials and limitations of any system written in dBASE II. This understanding gives managers and programmers a common ground for discussing the design and implementation of a computer system.

The programming novice will find that dBASE II can be fun if some time is devoted to study. This chapter assumes no prior programming experience. By working through examples which are successively harder, any reader may work up to more complex programming with enough practice. When the going gets too rough, it might be worthwhile to step back and re-try some of the more basic examples. With time, the solutions will seem more natural and understandable.

The more advanced programmers should still read this introductory chapter, since following chapters will build on these examples. Even the most knowledgeable dBASE II programmer will find new ideas which may prove invaluable later.

CHAPTER 3   INTRODUCTION TO PROGRAMMING

To give the dBASE II programmer a solid set of tools, standard program fragments will be introduced. These basic building blocks will be used repeatedly throughout all the programming examples. Such segments or modules may be used later by the programmer to build new applications. This modular approach will make programming and debugging a simpler task.

Creating a dBASE II program

A dBASE II program is simply a series of commands typed into a text file, similar to a letter which you would write with a word processor. Versions 2.3 and greater have a built-in editor for creating programs and our examples will make use of it.

Owners of earlier versions may use any CP/M word processor or text editor. Wordstar, Magic Wand, Mince and ED are all acceptable. A version of dBASE II with the built-in editor should be obtained as soon as possible.

If a word processor is used, several rules must be followed. The file name must have the ending of CMD, letting dBASE II know that it is a program file. If you own a 16 bit version of dBASE II, (i.e. IBM PC), an ending of PRG should be used for dBASE II programs. The word processor must also be told that the file is to be used for programming purposes and not as a text document.

With Wordstar, the file should be edited with the "N", or non-document mode. If the "D" mode is used, Wordstar will place characters in the file for its own use, and this will have unpredictable results when the program is run by dBASE II. Other word processors also have special program modes meeting this requirement.

This book does not give details on dBASE II's editor, as that is done thoroughly in the dBASE II manual. To begin to edit a CMD file the instruction MODIFY COMMAND filename is given. The CMD ending is not needed, as it will be added automatically. If the file named does not exist, the editor will create it. Otherwise, the existing file will be edited. The example programs will be shown in the text following the MODIFY statement. Listings of sample programs will be in **BOLD TYPE**. When you are finished entering the text of the program, press control-W, and dBASE II will save the program on the disk. To run the program tell dBASE II to DO the program.

Our first program will be called SAMPLE.CMD, and will perform some basic dBASE II functions.

. **MODIFY COMMAND SAMPLE**

```
* SAMPLE.CMD   12/1/82 ABG
USE MAIL
LIST
LIST LAST,CITY
REPORT FORM MAILLIST FOR CITY = "ARLINGTON"
```

The only new idea is the use of a comment in the first line of the program. This line starts with an asterisk, which means that any statements on the rest of the line will be ignored by dBASE II. The use of comments in a program is a necessary form of documentation, and an important habit to develop. Documentation helps the reader of the program and the programmer later. A common practice is to include the date of last modification and the authors name, giving someone to blame when the program doesn't work.

This program is just a set of commands, which would give the same results if typed into dBASE II individually. By putting them into a program file, we may repeat the series of functions by simply typing DO SAMPLE. To make the examples smaller, we will first DELETE Max Smith from the file.

. USE MAIL

. 1

. DELETE

00001 DELETION (S)

. PACK

PACK COMPLETE, 00002 RECORDS COPIED

. DO SAMPLE

```
00001  SALLY      FIELDS      30 W. ALEMEDA ST.   ST. LOUIS   MO 97821
00002  JIM        JONES       1 CENTER ST.        ARLINGTON   MA 02174
00001  FIELDS     ST. LOUIS
00002  JONES      ARLINGTON

       PAGE NO.  00001

                               MAILING LIST REPORT

           NAME                    CITY

       JIM        JONES        ARLINGTON
```

So what's the big deal? You could have typed that directly into dBASE II just as fast. Stick with it a while. We will soon produce some more useful programs.

Communicating from within a program

We often want our programs to ask questions, and then make appropriate responses. This is called "I/O", for input and output, by programmers. There are many ways to handle I/O from a dBASE II program, but we will just use the ? and ACCEPT commands for now.

The ? command has already been introduced, and may be translated as "what is the value of." It may be used to display the contents of a variable, or a statement in quotation marks. Multiple variables and statements may be displayed by separating each one with a comma.

```
. ? "HELLO"

HELLO

. ? "HELLO", "FRED"

HELLO  FRED

. STORE "JOE" TO NAME

. ? NAME

JOE

. ? "HELLO", NAME

HELLO JOE
```

The ACCEPT command is similar to STORE, in that it places any information entered into a memory variable. An additional feature is the ability to add a message, which is displayed when the input is requested. The colon before the input is provided by dBASE II.

```
. ACCEPT TO NAME

: FRED

. ? NAME

FRED
```

39

```
. ACCEPT "WHAT IS YOUR NAME?" TO NAME

WHAT IS YOUR NAME?: JON
```

Let's use the editor to create a program called SAMPLE2 to try these commands out.

```
. MODIFY COMMAND SAMPLE2

* SAMPLE2.CMD  12/1/82 ABG
ACCEPT "WHAT IS YOUR NAME" TO NAME
? NAME, "IS A LOVELY NAME!"


. DO SAMPLE2

WHAT IS YOUR NAME:DORIS
DORIS IS A LOVELY NAME!
```

You may now write in your resume, that you have written programs which involve interaction between computers and humans.

Writing a useful program

There are many more commands to learn before we can write complete programs. Rather than continuing with detailed explanations of each command, we will begin writing a useful label printing program. As new commands are needed, they will be introduced in the context of the label program.

Design the program first

Before writing any computer program, the requirements of the application should be analyzed. Before the computer is even turned on, you should write out the design in "pseudo code", a language which is close to English. The program may then be converted into a language the computer can understand.

We will number each line of the pseudo code for reference later in the chapter.

```
Design for Label Printing Program:
1. Use the mailing list file.
2. Read the first record.
3. Print the contents of the record in the following format:
        FIRST LAST
        ADDRESS
        CITY, STATE ZIP
```

4. Move to the next record.
5. Continue the process until all the names and addresses have
been printed.

<u>Version</u> <u>for</u> <u>one</u> <u>label</u>

The first three lines are simple to translate. Let's write
the first draft of LABEL.CMD to use just these lines. We will
also start using comments that describe the purpose of the
program.

. MODIFY COMMAND LABEL

*   LABEL.CMD 12/1/82 ABG VERSION 1
*   THIS PROGRAM WILL PRINT MAILING LABELS
*   FROM THE FILE MAIL.DBF
*
USE MAIL
? FIRST, LAST
? ADDRESS
? CITY,STATE,ZIP

. DO LABEL

SALLY   FIELDS
30 W. ALEMEDA ST.
ST. LOUIS MO 97821

As a first draft, this program works fairly well. The only
problem is the extra space between first and last name, and
between city and state.

This extra space is due to dBASE II's way of adding enough
blanks to fill a field. When told to display the field, it also
displays these blanks. The extra spaces may be removed, by having
dBASE II display the field with the TRIM function.

Let's modify the program and run it again.

. MODIFY COMMAND LABEL

*   LABEL.CMD 12/1/82 ABG   VERSION 2
*   THIS PROGRAM WILL PRINT MAILING LABELS
*   FROM THE FILE MAIL.DBF
*

41

```
USE MAIL
? TRIM(FIRST), LAST
? ADDRESS
? TRIM(CITY), STATE, ZIP


. DO LABEL

SALLY FIELDS
30 W. ALEMEDA ST.
ST. LOUIS MO 97821
```

That's good enough for now. To make the labels look better a comma should be added between city and state.

The code for steps 4 and 5 comes next. The SKIP command will have dBASE II move to the next record, but there is still no way of repeating the label printing commands until the end of the file is reached.

DO WHILE loop

A loop is needed. This is a programming technique for repeating a series of commands many times. dBASE II will let us create a DO WHILE loop for this type of procedure. In order for our program to print labels for all the records in the MAIL file, it must do two things. It must repeat the label printing commands after it SKIPs to the next record, and it must stop when the last record has been printed.

We will use the system variable EOF to tell our program when to quit. When dBASE II is told to SKIP past the last record, the DO WHILE loop will stop because EOF has been reached.

To continue the loop until EOF is true, we will start our loop with DO WHILE .NOT. EOF. This seems slightly backwards, but it is required by the dBASE II syntax. The periods around the word NOT are also a matter of syntax. At the end of our program we put ENDDO. This means that the program should return to the DO WHILE statement, and test for EOF again.

This type of loop is such a common programming practice that we will create a skeleton, or program fragment, to be used in many applications.

```
* DO WHILE FRAGMENT     12/1/82   ABG
* THIS FRAGMENT WILL BE USED WHENEVER WE NEED TO PROCESS
* A FILE ONE RECORD AT A TIME, UNTIL END OF THE FILE IS REACHED.
*
DO WHILE .NOT. EOF
```

```
     *
     * PROCESS THE RECORD
     *
     SKIP
ENDDO
```

Most programmers indent any instructions which are within a loop. This is only to make the program easier to read. Let's put this fragment into our label program, and print the labels again.

```
. MODIFY COMMAND LABEL

*   LABEL.CMD  12/1/82 ABG  VERSION 3
*   THIS PROGRAM WILL PRINT MAILING LABELS
*   FROM THE FILE MAIL.DBF
*
USE MAIL
DO WHILE .NOT. EOF
    ? TRIM(FIRST), LAST
    ? ADDRESS
    ? TRIM(CITY) - "," , STATE, ZIP
    SKIP
ENDDO


. DO LABEL

SALLY FIELDS
30 W. ALEMEDA ST.
ST. LOUIS, MO 97821
RECORD: 00002
JIM JONES
1 CENTER ST.
ARLINGTON, MA 02174
RECORD: 00002
```

Well, it's getting better, but still needs some work. Labels were printed for both records, and the program stopped after the last record. The only problem now is the "RECORD: 00002" after each label. The record number is printed by dBASE II every time it SKIPs.

This may be fixed, but first let's use it to tell us how the program worked. We'll follow the flow of the program in pseudo code again to make analysis easier.

1. Use the mailing list file.
2. Go to the first record.
3. Check to make sure that the end of the file hasn't been reached.

4. Print the label format.
5.   SKIP to the second record. DBASE II prints the new record
number when it SKIPs. This is why "RECORD: 0002" is printed.
6. Check for EOF.
7. Print a second label.
8. SKIP again. We can't SKIP past the end of the file, so we are
stuck at "RECORD: 0002" again.
9. Check for EOF. EOF is now true so the program stops.

       We   can   now see that EOF is only true when we try to SKIP
past the end of the file, not when the record pointer is at the
last record.

       The program is working correctly, but we don't want messages
like "RECORD: 0002" printed. These messages from dBASE II may be
turned off with the command SET TALK OFF.

       Another   change   is   to have each label separated by blank
lines. This is done with a single ? command, which means "print a
blank line." We will separate each label with three blank lines.
This is because most commercially available labels are six lines
long. When we start printing labels on the printer, we will want
only one record per label. The three lines for information and
three blanks will fit perfectly.

. MODIFY COMMAND LABEL

```
*   LABEL.CMD   12/1/82 ABG   VERSION 4
*   THIS PROGRAM WILL PRINT MAILING LABELS
*   FROM THE FILE MAIL.DBF

SET TALK OFF
USE MAIL
DO WHILE .NOT. EOF
    ? TRIM(FIRST), LAST
    ? ADDRESS
    ? TRIM(CITY) - "," , STATE, ZIP
    ?
    ?
    ?
    SKIP
ENDDO
```

. DO LABEL

SALLY FIELDS
30 W. ALEMEDA ST.
ST. LOUIS, MO 97821

```
JIM JONES
1 CENTER ST.
ARLINGTON, MA 02174
```

Sending the labels to the printer

Now that the label program works, some hard copy is needed.
Labels on a screen are not very useful. Turning the printer on
from a program simply requires the SET PRINT ON command. This
will cause anything shown on the screen to be sent to the
printer. Printing is stopped with the SET PRINT OFF command. That
is logical, isn't it?

```
. MODIFY COMMAND LABEL

*   LABEL.CMD  12/1/82 ABG  VERSION 5
*   THIS PROGRAM WILL PRINT MAILING LABELS
*   FROM THE FILE MAIL.DBF
*
SET TALK OFF
USE MAIL
SET PRINT ON
DO WHILE .NOT. EOF
   ? TRIM(FIRST), LAST
   ? ADDRESS
   ? TRIM(CITY) -  "," , STATE, ZIP
   ?
   ?
   ?
   SKIP
ENDDO
SET PRINT OFF
```

Did it work for you? It worked here.

Getting fancy with IF statements

Next we will modify our program so that it only prints
certain records. For instance, we can print labels for people who
live in a certain city, or zip code. A mailing list is only
useful if it can be used selectively.

Examining some figures from a sample mailing list will make
this clear. Suppose there are 5,000 names on a mailing list.
Each letter costs 15 cents in printing, 3 cents in labor, and 20

cents in postage, for a total of 38 cents per letter. Mailings
are made to this list every three months.

```
                    28
     $     0.38     per letter
     x 5000.00      letters
     ---------
        1900.00     per mailing
     x         4    mailings per year
     ---------
     $ 7600.00      per year
        5600.00
```

      If only 10 percent of these letters could have been
excluded, because of selections made on location or other
criteria, a savings of $760.00 could be realized in one year.
That would pay for your copy of dBASE II.

      These savings can be obtained with one little word, IF. This
command is used to tell dBASE II when to perform certain
operations.   The structure of the IF command is similar to the DO
WHILE. A condition is tested, and if it is found to be true, all
the commands between the IF and ENDIF are executed.

```
IF condition is true
perform any number of commands
ENDIF
```

By putting an IF construct in our label program, we may select
only certain records to be printed.

      Instead of changing our working label program, we will
retype the program under a new name, LAB-SEL.CMD.

```
. MODIFY COMMAND LAB-SEL

*   LAB-SEL 12/1/82 ABG VERSION1
*   THIS PROGRAM WILL PRINT MAILING LABELS
*   FROM THE FILE MAIL.DBF FOR SELECTED CITIES ONLY
*
SET TALK OFF
USE MAIL
SET PRINT ON
DO WHILE .NOT. EOF
    IF CITY = "ARLINGTON"
       ? TRIM(FIRST), LAST
       ? ADDRESS
       ? TRIM(CITY) - "," , STATE, ZIP
       ?
       ?
       ?
    ENDIF
```

```
    SKIP
ENDDO
SET PRINT OFF


. DO LAB-SEL

JIM JONES
1 CENTER ST.
ARLINGTON, MA 02174
```

The lines of the program, between the IF and ENDIF, were only executed for those records for which city is equal to ARLINGTON. We have just saved 50% of our postage cost.

Giving the user a choice

As long as we can print labels for selected criteria, why not let the user of the program decide which city to search for. We will have the program ask, with the ACCEPT command, which city to select for.

```
. MODIFY COMMAND LAB-SEL

*   LAB-SEL.CMD   12/1/82 ABG   VERSION 2
*   THIS PROGRAM WILL PRINT MAILING LABELS
*   FROM THE FILE MAIL.DBF AFTER ASKING
*   FOR THE CITY TO SELECT.
*
SET TALK OFF
USE MAIL
ACCEPT "FOR WHICH CITY SHOULD I PRINT LABELS?"  TO CHOICE
SET PRINT ON
DO WHILE .NOT. EOF
    IF CITY  = CHOICE
        ? TRIM(FIRST), LAST
        ? ADDRESS
        ? TRIM(CITY) - "," , STATE, ZIP
        ?
        ?
        ?
    ENDIF
    SKIP
ENDDO
SET PRINT OFF
```

. DO LAB-SEL

FOR WHICH CITY SHOULD I PRINT LABELS?:ST. LOUIS

SALLY FIELDS
30 W. ALEMEDA ST.
ST. LOUIS, MO 97821

Adding a menu

There are now two programs for printing labels, LABEL.CMD
and LAB-SEL.CMD. An experienced dBASE II user, such as yourself,
will be able to use either program with the DO command. If
someone else is to use our programs, they must either be trained
or have detailed instructions. A method should be provided for
new users to print labels without training in dBASE II.

The simplest approach is to use a menu at first. Once
everyone feels comfortable with dBASE II, they will be able to
move to the command driven method you now use.

Writing a menu program in dBASE II is a simple exercise. All
the menu program must do is clear the screen, present the choices
available, and allow the user to select one of those choices.
Once you have created a sample menu, you will know enough to
create one for most situations.

There are several new commands you must learn to write a
good menu. The first is ERASE, which simply clears the screen,
and is a valuable addition to any program. It is hard to read a
menu, if the screen is cluttered with text from previous
commands. Try putting ERASE in all your programs, whenever you
want to start again with a clean slate.

A loop is needed, which will present the menu repeatedly
until the user chooses to stop the program. A DO WHILE loop will
continue as long as the condition following the WHILE is true. We
use the statement, DO WHILE T, at the beginning of our program. T
is a system variable which is equal to true. The loop will thus
continue forever.

There are two ways to leave the loop. CANCEL will stop the
program, and return to dBASE. QUIT will stop, and return to CP/M.

With this menu program, we will introduce the practice of
including comments within the program as they are needed. This
will help you understand the program now, and later when it needs
to be updated.

```
-------------------------------------------------------------------
. MODIFY COMMAND MENU

* MENU.CMD     12/1/82   ABG    VERSION 1
* THIS PROGRAM WILL PRESENT THE VARIOUS LABEL
* MAKING OPTIONS. IT WILL ALSO OFFER ON-LINE HELP.

* PREVENT DBASE FROM SENDING EXTRA COMMENTS TO THE SCREEN
SET TALK OFF

* SET UP THE LOOP
DO WHILE T

* PRESENT THE MENU
  ERASE
  ?
  ?
  ? "-----------------------------------------------------------"
  ? "                    LABEL PRINTING MENU"
  ?
  ?
  ? "            1.   PRINT LABELS FOR ALL CITIES"
  ?
  ? "            2.   PRINT LABELS FOR SELECTED CITIES"
  ?
  ? "            3.   INSTRUCTIONS "
  ?
  ? "            4.   LEAVE THIS MENU, AND RETURN TO dBASE"
  ?
  ? "            5.   LEAVE THIS MENU, AND RETURN TO CP/M"
  ?                .
  ?

* FIND OUT WHAT THE USER WANTS TO DO
ACCEPT   "           WHAT SHOULD I DO NEXT" TO NEXT

*  DO WHAT THE USER TOLD YOU TO
IF NEXT = "1"
   DO LABEL
   * PRINT ALL THE LABELS
ENDIF

IF NEXT = "2"
   DO LAB-SEL
   * PRINT LABELS FOR SELECTED CITIES
ENDIF

IF NEXT = "3"
   DO HELP
   * PRESENT A SCREEN OF INSTRUCTIONS
ENDIF
```

```
IF NEXT = "4"
   CANCEL
   *   RETURN TO DBASE
ENDIF

IF NEXT = "5"
   QUIT
   *   RETURN TO CP/M
ENDIF

ENDDO
```

A menu program should have a standard structure. A screen full of options is presented, a selection is requested, and the proper program is run. A loop is placed around the whole program, so that it will continue until the user is finished making selections.

In order to start the menu program, the user may either start dBASE II and type DO MENU, or start the program from CP/M with the command DBASE MENU. Any dBASE II program may be run from CP/M.

Help is on the way

When writing the menu, a HELP program was included. Help should be available from every menu you write. It can present detailed instructions, or just give the name of a knowledgeable person to contact. Writing a help program is simple. All it must do is clear the screen, display some text, and then wait until the user wants to return to the menu.

```
.MODIFY COMMAND HELP

* HELP.CMD     12/1/82 ABG    VERSION 1
* PRESENTS A HELP SCREEN FOR THE LABEL
* MAKING PROGRAMS.
*

ERASE

* PLACE YOUR HELP MESSAGE HERE
?
?
?   "IF YOU HAVE ANY QUESTIONS, PLEASE CONTACT YOUR SUPERVISOR"
?
?
ACCEPT "PRESS RETURN TO CONTINUE" TO WAIT
```

CHAPTER 3   INTRODUCTION TO PROGRAMMING

The ACCEPT instruction is there so the screen will stay
until the return key is hit. The program will then return to
MENU.CMD. WAIT is called a "dummy" variable, because it doesn"t
really hold any useful information.

A few words on the DO command

DBASᵉ II allows one program to DO another. This is called
"program nesting". When one program runs another program, the
first one is said to "call" the second. When the called program
is finished, dBASE II will return to the program which first made
the DO call.

DO calls may be up to 16 levels deep in dBASE II, meaning
that a program can DO a program, which can DO a program, which
can DO a program, etc. Don't nest your programs too deeply,
because trying to figure them out later will be like looking into
a double set of mirrors.

Conclusion

If you followed all the examples in this chapter, you should
now have a fair understanding of what programming is like. It
is mostly an endless repetition of designing, writing code,
testing, more designing, more coding, and more testing. Now you
know why programmers make such fabulous salaries.

This chapter is the last one which is recommended for
novices. The rest of the book will move at a much faster pace.
The material covered to this point should be adequate preparation
for the next chapters, but you should also read the manual
thoroughly. It may be necessary to read some of the books on
programming listed in the bibliography, if the going gets rough.

CHAPTER 4

DEVELOPING STANDARD dBASE II TECHNIQUES

As you can tell from looking at the manual, we have only scratched the surface of dBASE II's language. As the introduction said, the purpose of this book is not to redefine every command, but to present a working subset.

This chapter will help enlarge this subset, by demonstrating many commonly used techniques in dBASE II programming. Unfortunately, these cover such a broad range of topics that a structured approach is too cumbersome. An attempt will be made to present new commands in the order in which they would appear in a program.

Again, these examples will be used in later chapters, so don't skip anything.

SETing up the working environment

The first thing any program should do is create the proper environment. This would include the way in which dBASE II appears to the user, as well as the data entry features available. The SET command will be used to turn many of these features either ON or OFF.

We have seen the SET TALK OFF command, which prevents dBASE II from sending messages to the screen on its own. Many SETs are involved with data entry, and they provide control over the way full screen data entry is done. Here is a partial list of these SET commands and the features they control:

SET	FEATURE
BELL ON/OFF	When ON, the terminal bell is rung when the end of the field is reached
CONFIRM ON/OFF	When ON, a carriage return must be entered to move to the next field.
INTENSITY ON/OFF	When ON, the terminal will display parts of the screen in inverse video.

Many of these parameters are a matter of personal taste, so the safest route is to leave most of them in their default positions at first. As you become more sure of dBASE II's operation, you should begin experimenting with the many SETs.

One new SET command, which is a blessing to long time dBASE II programmers, is SET ESCAPE OFF. In normal operation, pressing the escape key would stop any program being run. If this were to happen while a program was updating a file, the final condition of the file would be uncertain. When ESCAPE is SET OFF, the escape key will no longer have any effect. This command should not be given until a working program is finished. If ESCAPE is OFF when a program being developed goes into an infinite loop, or

some other problem is encountered, the only way out is to press
the reset button.

Built-in functions

     Many of the small tasks, which in other languages would
require a program to be written, are provided by dBASE II. These
small routines are called functions. A function will take an
expression or variable, and convert it into a new form.

     Most functions are given their arguments, the information to
work on, in parentheses. dBASE II then translates the function
and argument so that the result is the information in the desired
form.

     TRIM is a function we have already used. It will return the
contents of the specified field without the trailing blanks.

  . ? LAST, FIRST

SMITH   JOHN

  . ? TRIM(LAST), FIRST

SMITH JOHN

     Many functions give a result which is either true or false.
For example, FILE("filename") is true if the file named is found
on the disk. This function may be used by a program to test for
the existence of a data file.

     This type of true/false function may be used in an IF
statement to determine the next action to be taken. For instance:

```
IF FILE("MAIL.DBF")
     USE MAIL
ELSE
   ? "MAIL.DBF is not on the disk"
ENDIF
```


     If the file MAIL.DBF is present, the FILE function is true,
and MAIL will be USEd. The quotation marks are a matter of dBASE
syntax.

     The !() function will convert all the letters of a variable,
or statement in quotes, to capitals.

```
. ? !("hello")

HELLO
```

As more complex programs are written, the needed functions
will be introduced.

Multiple conditions

There are many occasions where more than one condition must
be tested by an IF or DO WHILE statement. The correct method is
to connect each condition with an .AND. or .OR. statement.   It
will also be helpful to determine if a condition is .NOT. true.
We have seen this in the command DO WHILE .NOT. EOF.

When the conditions become too complex,   it is often
required that they be separated by parentheses. Here is a short
example from our hypothetical inventory system:

LIST FOR VENDOR = "APPLE" .AND. (COST > 100 .AND. COST < 300)

This will only list those items manufactured by APPLE
Computer which cost between 100 and 300 dollars. It will take
some practice to become versatile with complex conditions.

Managing memory

When writing large systems involving many CMD files, proper
attention must be paid to management of the memory variables
used. There is a limit of 64 available memory variables, and care
must be taken to RELEASE variables when finished with them.
Otherwise memory may be filled before the program is finished.

Programs may save information in memory for the use of other
programs. Using this technique, one program may send messages and
results to another program. This is called "passing parameters."

In dBASE II, all memory variables are available to be used
and modified by every program. This is as dangerous as it is
convenient. The programmer must be careful when changing a
variable in one program, if the same variable name is used in
other programs.

A common practice is to RELEASE variables which a program
creates, and put memory back into its original state, before
leaving the program. Many small modules may then be
interconnected without the fear of unexpected changes in memory
variables.

A <u>CASE</u> <u>of</u> <u>IFs</u>, <u>please</u>

In certain types of programs, such as menu programs, it is common to find a whole series of IF statements. Each IF will handle one possible function on the menu. A powerful command in dBASE II is the DO CASE statement, which is perfect for handling this kind of multiple condition situation. The DO CASE syntax is similar to that of the DO WHILE statement.

DO CASE

CASE condition 1
statements

CASE condition 2
statements

CASE condition N
statements

OTHERWISE
statements

ENDCASE

Many CASEs may be checked, and each condition is tested in turn. When a condition is found to be true, all the statements are performed until another CASE if reached. Only one case may be found to be true. After the first true CASE is finished, the next instruction to be performed will be following the ENDCASE statement. If none of the conditions are true, the OTHERWISE is performed. The OTHERWISE command is optional.

Let's MODIFY our menu program of the last chapter to use the DO CASE statement.

. MODIFY COMMAND MENU

* MENU.CMD   12/1/82 ABG   VERSION 2
* THIS PROGRAM WILL PRESENT THE VARIOUS LABEL
* MAKING OPTIONS. IT WILL ALSO OFFER ON-LINE HELP.

* PREVENT DBASE FROM SENDING EXTRA COMMENTS TO THE SCREEN
SET TALK OFF

* SET UP THE LOOP
DO WHILE T

* PRESENT THE MENU
    ERASE

```
?
?
? "-----------------------------------------------------------------"
? "                        LABEL PRINTING MENU"
?
?
? "            1.   PRINT LABELS FOR ALL CITIES"
?
? "            2.   PRINT LABELS FOR SELECTED CITIES"
?
? "            3.   INSTRUCTIONS "
?
? "            4.   LEAVE THIS MENU, AND RETURN TO dBASE II"
?
? "            5.   LEAVE THIS MENU, AND RETURN TO CP/M"
?
?

* FIND OUT WHAT THE USER WANTS TO DO
ACCEPT   "         WHAT SHOULD I DO NEXT" TO NEXT

*   DO WHAT THE USER WANTS
DO CASE

CASE NEXT = "1"
    DO LABEL
    * PRINT ALL THE LABELS

CASE NEXT = "2"
    DO LAB-SEL
    * PRINT LABELS FOR SELECTED CITIES

CASE NEXT = "3"
    DO HELP
    * PRESENT A SCREEN OF INSTRUCTIONS

CASE NEXT = "4"
    CANCEL
    *   RETURN TO DBASE

CASE NEXT = "5"
    QUIT
    *   RETURN TO CP/M

ENDCASE

ENDDO
```

The   DO   CASE   statement makes programs easier to   read   and
write. Our programs will use it extensively.

More detail on DO WHILE loops

Applications often require that a program repeat a procedure a certain number of times, or while a condition is true. The DO WHILE .NOT. EOF is a typical looping condition. We will briefly describe some common methods of controlling loops.

LOOP CONDITION	PURPOSE
DO WHILE T	This type of loop is often used for the outer loop of a main menu program. It is known as an infinite loop, because T will always be true. The only way out is to stop the program with a QUIT command.
DO WHILE .NOT. EOF	This controls programs which must process one record at a time, until the end of the file is reached.
STORE T TO MORE DO WHILE MORE	A variable is created to control the loop. When it is necessary to exit the loop, MORE is set to F or false. The next time MORE is tested the loop will end.
STORE 0 TO COUNTER DO WHILE COUNTER < 10	We sometimes want a loop to repeat an exact number of times. A variable, such as COUNTER, is created. Each time a required task is completed, COUNTER will be increased by one. When the desired number of passes have been completed, and COUNTER becomes equal to 10, the loop will stop.

It is recommended that standard loops be used throughout your dBASE II programs. This will increase writing speed, and make understanding the program easier.

It is possible to "nest" DO WHILE loops, which means that one loop may be within another. It is essential that each loop stay completely within the other. Here is an example of a correctly nested loop:

```
DO WHILE T
   DO WHILE .NOT. EOF
      ? LAST
      SKIP
   ENDDO
ENDDO
```

The indentation at each level of DO loop is not required, but it helps keep the nesting order straight. Improperly nested loops will have unpredictable results.

Creating data entry forms

One of the nicest features of dBASE II programming is the ability to create forms on the screen which look exactly like the the original documents. There is full screen editing available, just as in the EDIT and APPEND commands. It is helpful when many records must be added.

The form is created by entering the position on the terminal's screen for each piece of information to be displayed. A normal terminal has 24 lines of 80 characters each. Like most programming languages, dBASE II starts counting at 0, so the top line on the screen is line 0. dBASE II reserves this line for its own use. Columns are counted from 0 to 79, so the first character is displayed at column 0.

The @ SAY command, pronounced as "at say", is used to enter these coordinates. The line position is given first, followed by the column position. To place the word "HELLO" on the first available line and the 10th column position, the following command would be used:

@ 1,9 SAY "HELLO"

The column position is 9 because counting starts at 0. The command @ SAY tells dBASE II to simply print the text that follows. If we had wanted to allow data to be entered to a variable at that position, we would have used the @ GET command.

If memory variables are used in the form, they must be initialized with STORE commands. This will tell dBASE II their type and how much data they will hold.

Once the variables are initialized and the screen positions defined, the READ command is given and the form is displayed on the terminal. You may move the cursor to and enter data into any GET field. When the last field is passed, all of the data entered will remain in the variables used in the GETs. Here is a sample set of commands which will display a simple data entry form.

```
. MODIFY COMMAND SCREEN1

STORE "                      " TO name
STORE "                          " TO address
STORE "              " TO city
STORE "   " TO state
STORE "       " TO zip
@ 4,4    SAY "Name"
@ 4,20   GET name
@ 6,4    SAY "Address"
@ 6,20   GET address
```

```
@ 8,4    SAY "City"
@ 8,11   GET city
@ 8,25   SAY "State"
@ 8,33   GET state
@ 8,45   SAY "ZIP"
@ 8,50   GET zip
READ
```

. DO SCREEN1

    Name   :   :

    Address   :   :

    City   :   : State   : :   Zip :   :

     The forms creation feature is one of dBASE II's major
advantages over a language like BASIC. A simple READ command
provides full screen editing.

ZIP

     Although the @ SAY and @ GET commands are extremely
powerful, it can be a slow process to create a complex form. To
simplify that task a program called ZIP is provided with dBASE
II. ZIP is a dBASE II program generator, which means it can write
dBASE II programs to your specifications.

     The programs that ZIP writes include all the @ SAY and @ GET
statements needed to present a complete form in dBASE II. All you
have to do is run ZIP from CP/M, type your form on the screen,
and tell ZIP to write the program. The program is written on the
disk, ready to run from dBASE II. Detailed instructions on ZIP's
operation can be found in the dBASE II manual.

     There are a few rules to follow with ZIP. To have text
appear in a @ SAY statement, just type the text onto the screen.
You must preceed variables with a @ for @ SAY statements, and a #
for @ GET statements.

     When you tell ZIP to write the program, it produces three
files; a ZIP file which contains a copy of your form for future
modification, a ZPR file which is a printable copy of your screen
for documentation purposes, and a CMD or FMT file which contains
the @ SAY and @ GET statements for the form.

Once the program is completed, you can start up dBASE II and use the new program as if you had written it yourself. Here is a sample form, followed by the dBASE II program produced by ZIP.

```
=================================================
!                                               !
!     Name : #name                              !
!                                               !
!     Address : #address                        !
!                                               !
!     City : #city                              !
!                                               !
!     State : #state       Zip : #zip           !
!                                               !
!                                               !
!                                               !
=================================================
```

Please Enter Name And Address

```
@  0,15 SAY "================================================="
@  1,15 SAY "!                                               !"
@  2,15 SAY "!     Name :"
@  2,26 GET name
@  2,58 SAY "!"
@  3,15 SAY "!                                               !"
@  4,15 SAY "!     Address :"
@  4,29 GET address
@  4,58 SAY "!"
@  5,15 SAY "!                                               !"
@  6,15 SAY "!     City :"
@  6,26 GET city
@  6,58 SAY "!"
@  7,15 SAY "!                                               !"
@  8,15 SAY "!     State :"
@  8,27 GET state
@  8,39 SAY "Zip :"
@  8,45 GET zip
@  8,58 SAY "!"
@  9,15 SAY "!                                               !"
@ 10,15 SAY "!                                               !"
@ 11,15 SAY "!                                               !"
@ 12,15 SAY "================================================="
@ 14,21 SAY "Please Enter Name And Address"
```

This program was created in less than 5 minutes with ZIP. If it becomes necessary to change it, you could have ZIP read it back from the disk and then produce a new edited version.

Unfortunately, the versions of dBASE II for the 16 bit computers do not yet include ZIP. This should change in a few months.

Saving forms in a FMT file

Instead of saving the @ SAY and @ GET commands in a CMD file, they may be saved in a FMT file. This is like a CMD file, but contains no other statements than the @ SAY and @ GETs. To display a form in a CMD file you must DO that file. To use a FMT file just tell dBASE II to SET FORMAT TO the file. When a READ statement is given, the form defined in either program will be displayed.

The distinction between the two methods of displaying forms is a fine one, and is mostly a matter of personal taste. You should experiment with both techniques.

Sending forms to the printer

A form which has been created for display on the terminal, may also be sent to a printer. The command SET PRINT ON will cause all @ SAY statements to be sent to the printer. Any @ GET statements will be ignored, and not sent to the printer.

The usual way to use the printer is to create a version of the form for the screen, and then convert all @ GETs to @ SAYs. This will allow the same form to be appear on the screen and the printer.

Pretty as a PICTURE

There is an option available with the @ GET command, which is called the PICTURE clause. This will define a format for displaying and entering data on the screen.

A common example is entering the date. This has often plagued programmers, because it is so difficult to get people to enter a date in the correct format. Should they use Jan. 1, 1982, or 1/1/82, or 01-01-82, etc.

If this statement is included in a program, @ 10,20 GET DATE PICTURE "99/99/99", the field for date will be displayed in the following format:

                    : / / :

Only numbers may be typed in the blank spaces, entering a character will only cause a beep from the terminal. In addition, the / symbols may not be typed over. The only possible format for the date is obvious.

The type of data allowed in a field is determined by the character in the PICTURE command. In the previous example a 9 was used, which only allows numbers to be entered. The ! sign will automatically convert any input to upper case characters. This will be used in many of our menu programs. The other PICTURE characters are defined in the dBASE II manual.

WAITing for a single character

Many programs, such as menus, make single key entry of commands desirable. This means that the return key does not have to be pressed to complete an entry.

The   dBASE II command for this single key entry is WAIT TO. WAIT is similar to ACCEPT, but only one character may be entered and no prompt may be displayed. The character entered is stored in a memory variable.

```
-----------------------------------------------------------------
. WAIT TO NEXT

WAITING A

. ? NEXT

A
-----------------------------------------------------------------
```

The ability to use single key entry is nice, but the message WAITING, is ugly. A tricky way to prevent it from being displayed is to SET CONSOLE OFF before WAITing. When CONSOLE is SET OFF nothing will be shown on the screen, but the keyboard may still receive input. The following lines of code will allow single key entry without any WAITING message reaching the screen:

```
SET CONSOLE OFF
WAIT TO NEXT
SET CONSOLE ON
```

If it is not necessary to store the input in a variable, WAIT may be used alone.

```
SET CONSOLE OFF
WAIT
SET CONSOLE ON
```

     This is commonly done to cause a program to stop until a key
is pressed.

The art of debugging, or why the hell did it do that?

     A fact of life for programmers is the occurrence of bugs.
Programming in dBASE II is easier than most languages, but it is
still possible to make mistakes. Luckily, there are excellent
debugging tools available.

     There are two SETs, ECHO and STEP, which provide most of the
debugging capability. When ECHO is SET ON, any command in a CMD
file is displayed on the screen as it is performed. STEP allows
the program to be performed one line at a time. STEP also offers
the choice of performing the next step, or entering a command
directly from the keyboard.

     When both ECHO and STEP are SET ON, a program may be run one
line at a time, and studied as it works out the logic of the
program. At any point, the program may be stopped and variables
checked or new commands entered. This is similar to using a
monitor program to debug assembly language instructions.

     Let's write a small sample program and use these commands to
study it.

```
--------------------------------------------------------------------
. MODIFY COMMAND TEST

USE MAIL
LIST LAST
ACCEPT "NAME A CITY ANY CITY" TO KEY
LIST FOR CITY = KEY


. DO TEST

00001  FIELDS
00002  JONES
NAME A CITY ANY CITY:ARLINGTON
00002  JIM        JONES        1 CENTER ST.        ARLINGTON  MA 02174
--------------------------------------------------------------------
```

     If we SET ECHO ON, we can see each line of the dBASE II
program as it is performed. Both the lines of the program, and
the results of those lines will appear on the screen.

```
--------------------------------------------------------------------
. SET ECHO ON
```

```
. DO TEST
DO TEST
USE MAIL
LIST LAST
00001  FIELDS
00002  JONES
ACCEPT "NAME A CITY ANY CITY" TO KEY
NAME A CITY ANY CITY:ARLINGTON
LIST FOR CITY = KEY
00002  JIM        JONES       1 CENTER ST.        ARLINGTON  MA 02174
```

     When we also SET STEP ON, each line of the program may be
studied in detail. Typing Y lets the program continue, and typing
N makes it stop for one command.

```
. SET STEP ON

SET STEP ON

. DO TEST

DO TEST
SINGLE STEP  Y:=STEP,  N:=KEYBOARD CMD,  ESC:=CANCELY

USE MAIL
SINGLE STEP  Y:=STEP,  N:=KEYBOARD CMD,  ESC:=CANCELY

LIST LAST
00001  FIELDS
00002  JONES
SINGLE STEP  Y:=STEP,  N:=KEYBOARD CMD,  ESC:=CANCELY

ACCEPT "NAME A CITY ANY CITY" TO KEY
NAME A CITY ANY CITY:ARLINGTON
SINGLE STEP  Y:=STEP,  N:=KEYBOARD CMD,  ESC:=CANCELN
```

     By typing N, we may now enter a command directly from the
keyboard. For instance, we might want to check the contents of
the variable KEY.

```
. LIST MEMORY

LIST MEMORY
KEY           (C)  ARLINGTON
** TOTAL **       01 VARIABLES USED  00009 BYTES USED
```

CHAPTER 4   DEVELOPING STANDARD dBASE II TECHNIQUES

```
SINGLE STEP  Y:=STEP,  N:=KEYBOARD CMD,  ESC:=CANCELY

LIST FOR CITY = KEY
00002 JIM       JONES       1 CENTER ST.      ARLINGTON  MA 02174
------------------------------------------------------------------
```

If it is necessary to obtain a printed copy of this debugging session, DEBUG may be SET ON. This sends the echoed lines only to the printer, and prevents the screen from being obscured by lines of the program.

Standard program structure

The best way to cure bugs is to prevent them. A standard format for your programs should be developed early. These good habits will make writing a dBASE II program a more natural procedure.

Here is an outline of a format which has proved successful. This should be used until one better suited to your programming style may be developed.

* Comments -- Name   Date   Author   Purpose of the program

Initialize screen format and variables

Set up a loop, if one is needed

    Present screen or menu of options

    Get user input

    Process the input and perform the appropriate function

 Loop back again until finished

Release any variables created in this DO file

Restore memory to the way it was when this program started

Conclusion

We are now ready to enter the real world of applications programming. The rest of the book will help you write programs which use the commands and techniques covered so far. This is probably a good time to quickly review the preceding chapters.

CHAPTER 5

DESIGNING A COMPLETE dBASE II SYSTEM

Turn off your computer

So far you have been using the computer to try out all the
examples. You have been working out the examples, haven't you?
The time has arrived to solve a complete application with dBASE
II, and the first action to take when approaching a new program
is to turn off the computer.

Take the time to think about the application, and create a
sound design for the solution. The design should include details
on the size and structure of your files, types of reports to be
printed, and pseudo code for all the programs to be written.
After all, would you buy a house that was built without a
blueprint?

What kind of programs should we write?

The dBASE II manual offers a complete accounting system
written in the dBASE II language. The problem with this technique
of teaching programming, is that the complexity of the
accounting system used in the examples obscures the programming
principles being demonstrated. The reader ends up saying, "now
why is the program posting the checks to this file, before a
report is written on some other file?"

We will take a different approach, and use an application
that is so simple that the standard programming practices will
stand out more clearly. Once these techniques become clear, you
will be able to apply them to more complex problems.

The sample application we will create is a college alumni
mailing list, but the programs may easily be modified for many
other uses. Most applications perform the same operations on a
set of files; adding, deleting, editing, finding, and printing
records. There is also a need to write custom reports, and
programs which link several files together.

Each program will be written as an independent module, which
performs only one logical function. If the modules are planned
and documented carefully, they may be reused for other
applications. This will allow future programs to be written by
joining previously tested modules.

Simple mailing list system

Story Book University is a small school of arts and
sciences. Like many other universities, its primary purpose is to
collect contributions from its alumni. To accomplish this, it has
a staff of clerks, whose sole job is to maintain a mailing list

of the alumni. Besides keeping the addresses of the alumni up to
date, (so that the contribution requests will reach them), each
contribution must be matched with the contributing alumni's
record.

The clerks would like a computer to perform much of their
work for them. Of greatest importance are the more tedious tasks,
such as removing duplicate entries from the files, printing
mailing labels, and cross referencing the contributions.

Analyze the work flow of the application

We must first analyze the way the data is processed. This
includes the amount of data to be entered, the frequency of
changes and deletions, and the computer background of the future
users of the program. If these factors are not considered, it is
entirely possible to write a program which performs the desired
functions in a manner which is more difficult than the existing
manual system.

New alumni and contributions will be entered at regular
intervals, and in large batches. Once they have been entered,
they must be verified for accuracy. During this review process
there should be a quick means of correcting any new entries.

The users will also want to search through the data base,
and update previously entered data. At times they will want to
simply scan through the file without any specific alumni in mind.

At regular intervals mailing labels will have to be
produced in zip code order to take advantage of bulk mailing
rates. A master listing of all alumni in last name order will
also be needed.

A report must list the contributions of every alumni, and
give subtotals for each graduating class. Another report is
needed to cross reference every contribution made by each alumni.

The users of this system will most likely be people who are
unfamiliar with computers. It should not be required that they
all learn a new language to perform their job. It appears that
the menu driven approach offers the most promise. The more
sophisticated users will still be able to use dBASE II to create
their own impromptu reports in the alumni data base.

When large volumes of data are involved, it is often
desirable to use data entry screens which resemble the form of
the original data. The program should present the same form for
as many functions as possible. Adjusting to the new system will
then be as painless as possible.

How fast must the programs be?

The example programs will not be designed with maximum speed in mind. The emphasis will be on writing programs which are as easy to read and understand as possible. It is always easier to speed up a well written program, than to understand and modify a program which was made cryptic in an attempt to write "tight" code.

How much of the application should we solve?

To make these introductory programs as clear as possible, we will only maintain the alumni name and address portion of the mailing list system.   A second section, which handles the individual contributions, may be added by the reader.

While as much of the system as possible should be considered in the original design, the addition of a new set of programs later will be a realistic example of the evolution of any computer system.

Pseudo code for a single file mailing list

Let's create an overall design of the system in pseudo code. This broad description will be followed by a series of refinements. If the resulting pseudo code is written in enough detail, it may quickly be translated into dBASE II code. This is similar to writing a book from an outline.

As sections of the system are introduced, the name of a CMD file which will perform that function will be printed. The chapters which follow will add more detail to the design, and then present the finished dBASE II program.

1) Present a sign-on message.   (SIGN-ON)
    This will allow a copyright to be displayed, and will give the user something to read while the program is starting up.

2) Initialize the system.   (INIT)
    This should be done at the start of the program, so that any files or variables which the entire system will use may be defined in one location.

3) Perform one of the following actions until the user is finished with the system.   (MAIN)

        4) Display the current record   (MAIN)
                If it has been marked for deletion, then show
                that fact on the screen   (DELCHECK)

5) The following actions may be taken on the current
   record:

      Delete the record   (DELETE)
      Edit the record   (EDIT)
      Print the record   (PRINT)

6) Other records may be seen in the following ways:

      Move backward through the file   (MAIN)
      Move forward through the file   (MAIN)
      Search for a specific record   (SEARCH)

7) Display helpful instructions on the system
                                               (HELP)

8) Present a selection of operations for maintenance of
   the alumni file: (MAINTAIN)

      Remove duplicates from the file   (DUPCHECK)
                                       (DUPREM)
      Verify new entries   (VERIFNEW)
      Verify deleted records   (VERIFDEL)
      Purge deleted records   (PURGE)
      Add default values for data entry (DEFAULTS)
      Backup the data files   (BACKUP)

9) Present the following choice of reports: (REPORT)

      Print labels for each alumni   (LABEL)
      Print a report on each alumni which lists the
      total contribution, and offers subtotals for each
      graduating class.   (CONTRIB.FRM)
      Print the complete record of each alumni
                                     (TOT-REP)

10) Leave the program and return to CP/M

Define the data structure

Before starting dBASE II and creating a DBF file, a "data
dictionary" should be established. This is simply a table which
lists the name, type, size, and description of each distinct data
item.

The process of building this list is as important as the
finished product. It could be discovered that certain items of
information are more useful when split into several pieces, while
other apparently unrelated items may be consolidated into one.

The list may then be used to create the files used by dBASE
II to store the data. The dBASE II conventions of data types and
sizes will be used to make this conversion process easier.

Name	Type	Size	Description
Id number	N	5	A unique number which is assigned to each alumni to assure correct identification.
First name	C	10	By separating the alumni's name between first and last, the last name may be used for sorting purposes.
Last name	C	15	
Address	C	25	Since this will usually be the alumni's home address, a separate company name is not necessary.
City	C	15	
State	C	2	
Zip code	C	5	This will be enough space for now. If the postal service has its way, the file structure may be modified to allow nine characters.
Phone number	C	14	Room must be left for the parenthesis around the area code and the hyphen with the number.
Year of Graduation	C	2	
Lifetime Contribution	N	10	If anyone contributes more than $9,999,999.99 the school can buy a new computer.
New alumni	L	1	This is a logical field which may be either true or false, (T or F). It will be used to mark a record as a new entry.

Which fields should be INDEXed

dBASE II will automatically maintain up to seven indices on any one file. When a record is APPENDed or EDITed, each of the indices will be updated. Unfortunately, every additional INDEX will cause this updating process to become slower.

When assigning INDEX files, the frequency of use for each INDEX should be considered. INDEX files which are rarely used should be created as the need arises. Instead of slowing down data entry for the entire program, it might be better to wait five to ten minutes when a rare report is run.

Since our mailing list is designed for a high volume of data entry, only the three most important fields will be INDEXed. Last name must be INDEXed to allow the search module to FIND a selected alumni. INDEXing on zip code is necessary for printing labels and the contribution report must be printed in order by year of graduation.

Establish documentation standards

Before the temptation to start writing code becomes too great, some attention should be paid to the form and style of the programs. Many programmers write the programs first, and then go back and add comments. This method is fine for a small, single person project, but the first large system will end up taking much longer than it should.

A properly documented program should not only run well, but should be written to be understandable to any other programmer. Even if you never show the programs to another soul, programs you have written will appear totally new in a few months.

One worthwhile test is to read the program aloud to another programmer. If you can't explain it clearly, than it probably isn't written well.

Several standards have been developed for dBASE II, as well as other languages. Try to use these until you develop your own:

   Start every program with a comment line which
   includes; the program name, programmer's initials,
   and date of last modification.

   Enter all dBASE II commands in upper case,
   and variable names in lower case.

   Indent all instructions within a DO loop or
   IF...ENDIF construct.

   Use standard variables names to control loops,
   and accept input.

   Leave blank lines between logical groups of
   instructions.

   Enter comments whenever a new function is begun.

Maintaining a documentation book

Once you start writing these beautifully documented programs, it is a good practice to maintain a notebook which

contains the latest version of each program. The simplest method
is to print a copy once a week of any newly created or modified
program. The book should also contain copies of the structure of
any data base file, as well as any reports which the system
produces. The first time you need to make a modification to the
system, you will be grateful for having done the extra work.

dUTIL

    If these rules sound like more trouble than they are worth,
have no fear. Fox and Geller Associates have written dUTIL to
simplify the lives of the dBASE II programmer.

    dUTIL, (pronounced DEE U TIL), will automatically format any
dBASE II CMD files according to the conventions established. It
will capitalize all dBASE II commands, convert all comments and
variables to lower case, and add the proper indentation. While it
is "pretty printing" the CMD file, it will also check for
matching DO WHILE...ENDDOs and IF...ENDIFs.   The programs in the
following chapters will be processed with dUTIL before they are
included.

Start a user's manual early

    This is the part of every computer system which is always
done last. Since programming projects are always late, the user's
manual often goes unwritten until long after the system is
installed.

    The manual should contain samples of all the menus, and a
description of each function of the system. Sample reports are
especially helpful. Unless you enjoy personally explaining each
function to every new user of the system, you should try to
finish the users manual at the same time as the program.

CHAPTER 6

CREATE THE DATA BASE AND SCREEN FILES

<u>Turn</u> <u>your</u> <u>computer</u> <u>on</u>

It's time to start dBASE II, and set up the DBF file and the index files for the mailing list.

A>dBASE

. CREATE

ENTER FILENAME: ALUMNI

ENTER RECORD STRUCTURE AS FOLLOWS:
```
FIELD    NAME,TYPE,WIDTH,DECIMAL PLACES
 001        ID:NO,N,5
 002        FIRST,C,10
 003        LAST,C,10
 004        ADDRESS,C,20
 005        CITY,C,10
 006        STATE,C,2
 007        ZIP,C,5
 008        PHONE,C,14
 009        YEAR:GRAD,C,2
 010        TOT:CONT,N,10,2
 011        NEW,L,1
 012        <CR>
```
INPUT DATA NOW? N

. USE ALUMNI

. APPEND

RECORD 00001

```
ID:NO       : 1
FIRST       : JOHN
LAST        : JONES
ADDRESS     : 17 SOUTH ST.
CITY        : WATERTOWN
STATE       : MA
ZIP         : 02156
PHONE       : 536-4546
YEAR:GRAD   : 68
TOT:CONT    : 100
NEW         : T
```

RECORD 00002

```
ID:NO       : 2
FIRST       : SALLY
LAST        : LADD
```

```
ADDRESS    : 14 CONGRESS ST.
CITY       : BOSTON
STATE      : MA
ZIP        : 02126
PHONE      : 742-5598
YEAR:GRAD  : 80
TOT:CONT   : 300
NEW        : T

RECORD 00003

ID:NO      : 3
FIRST      : SAM
LAST       : SMITH
ADDRESS    : 38 BOYLSTON ST.
CITY       : CAMBRIDGE
STATE      : MA
ZIP        : 02235
PHONE      : 492-5679
YEAR:GRAD  : 80
TOT:CONT   : 30
NEW        : T

RECORD 00004

ID:NO      : 4
FIRST      : RAY
LAST       : WATERS
ADDRESS    : 92 ST. BOTOLPH ST.
CITY       : BOSTON
STATE      : MA
ZIP        : 02234
PHONE      : 266-1982
YEAR:GRAD  : 69
TOT:CONT   : 0
NEW        : T

RECORD 00005

ID:NO      : <CR>

. INDEX ON !(LAST) TO LAST

. INDEX ON ZIP TO ZIP

. INDEX ON YEAR:GRAD TO YEAR
```

The last name field was INDEXed on !(LAST). This stores the
contents of LAST in the INDEX file as all capital letters. dBASE
II will treat lower case letters as distinct from upper case. If

a name is entered as Smith, FIND SMITH will not work. By creating
an INDEX on the capitalized version of LAST, and FINDing with a
capitalized key you will always find the right alumni.

Conventions for documenting forms

All of the forms in the programs were created with ZIP as
FMT files. The code which follows each screen may be entered by
hand, if you don't have a copy of ZIP. Several conventions for
describing forms have ben defined by ZIP. A variable which is
used in a @ SAY command is preceded by "@" and "#" defines a
variable for a @ GET.

To make the screens easier to read, all variables are shown
in **BOLD FACE**.

Creating general purpose forms

A form should be as generalized as possible. This will
allow a single FMT file to be used by many programs. If any
modifications must be made in the programs, a change to the FMT
file will affect the rest of the system.

Several standard variables names are used by the forms. MODE
shows which program is being run. DELETED shows when the current
record has been marked for deletion. PROMPT1, PROMPT2, and
PROMPT3 display messages. If the message must be changed, the
variables can be easily redefined in the program. COMMAND is a
standard variable name, which will be used in all the programs to
GET the next function to perform.

Using field names in forms

If a field name is used in a @ SAY statement, dBASE II will
SAY the value of that field from the current record. In a @ GET
statement the current record's value will be placed in the form,
and you may then change it. Whatever is left on the form when the
READ is complete will be written back into the file.

A common dBASE II programming technique is to STORE a
field's contents to a memory variable, and then GET the
variable. When the READ is over, the memory variable is REPLACEd
into the field. This technique allows the programmer to examine,
and possibly reject, the data before placing it in the file. To
make it clear to the reader of the programs that this is being
done, the memory variable used in the @ GET is commonly named
with a letter m followed by the field name.

FMT files used in the sample programs

GETDATA.FMT is used to add or edit records. This form uses memory variables for @ GETs. It is used in ADD.CMD and EDIT.CMD

MAINTAIN.FMT is the menu form for MAINTAIN.CMD.

REPORT.FMT is the menu form for REPORT.CMD.

SAYDATA.FMT is used to display the current record. The actual field names are used in the @ SAY statements. This is used in MAIN.CMD, VERIFYDEL.CMD, and VERFIYNEW.CMD.

TWOSHOW.FMT displays two records at one time, and is used to compare duplicate records in DUPREM.CMD.

GETDATA.FMT

Screen image:

```
                                @mode
    +============================================================+
    !                                                            !
    !    ID Number #mid:no                        @deleted       !
    !                                                            !
    !    First #mfirst              Last #mlast                  !
    !                                                            !
    !    Address #maddress                                       !
    !                                                            !
    !    City #mcity            State #mstate    Zip #mzip       !
    !                                                            !
    !    Phone #mphone                                           !
    !                                                            !
    !    Year Graduated #myear:grad  Contributions #mtot:cont   !
    !                                                            !
    !                                                            !
    +============================================================+
    !    @prompt1                                                !
    !    @prompt2                                                !
    !    @prompt3                                                !
    !                                                            !
    +============================================================+
```

dBASE II code:

```
@  1,27 SAY mode
@  2, 5 SAY "+============================================================+"
@  3, 5 SAY "!                                                            !"
@  4, 5 SAY "!    ID Number"
@  4,19 GET mid:no
@  4,51 SAY deleted
@  4,63 SAY "!"
@  5, 5 SAY "!                                                            !"
@  6, 5 SAY "!    First"
@  6,15 GET mfirst
@  6,33 SAY "Last"
@  6,38 GET mlast
@  6,63 SAY "!"
@  7, 5 SAY "!                                                            !"
@  8, 5 SAY "!    Address"
@  8,17 GET maddress
@  8,63 SAY "!"
@  9, 5 SAY "!                                                            !"
@ 10, 5 SAY "!    City"
@ 10,14 GET mcity
@ 10,29 SAY "State"
```

```
@ 10,35 GET mstate
@ 10,45 SAY "Zip"
@ 10,49 GET mzip
@ 10,63 SAY "!"
@ 11, 5 SAY "!                                                        !"
@ 12, 5 SAY "!     Phone"
@ 12,15 GET mphone
@ 12,63 SAY "!"
@ 13, 5 SAY "!                                                        !"
@ 14, 5 SAY "!     Year Graduated"
@ 14,24 GET myear:grad
@ 14,36 SAY "Contributions"
@ 14,49 GET mtot:cont
@ 14,63 SAY "!"
@ 15, 5 SAY "!                                                        !"
@ 16, 5 SAY "!                                                        !"
@ 17, 5 SAY "+====================================================+"
@ 18, 5 SAY "!"
@ 18, 8 SAY prompt1
@ 18,63 SAY "!"
@ 19, 5 SAY "!"
@ 19, 8 SAY prompt2
@ 19,63 SAY "!"
@ 20, 5 SAY "!"
@ 20, 8 SAY prompt3
@ 20,63 SAY "!"
@ 21, 5 SAY "!                                                        !"
@ 22, 5 SAY "+====================================================+"
```

MAINTAIN.FMT

Screen image:

```
+=================================================================+
!                                                                 !
!                    FILE   MAINTENANCE   MENU                    !
+=================================================================+
!                                                                 !
!              1. Find and remove duplicate entries               !
!                                                                 !
!              2. Verify new entries                              !
!                                                                 !
!              3. Verify entries marked for deletion              !
!                                                                 !
!              4. Remove entries marked for deletion              !
!                                                                 !
!              5. Enter default values for new entries            !
!                                                                 !
!              6. Quit to PIP.COM for file backup                 !
!                                                                 !
!              7. Return to main menu                             !
!                                                                 !
!              Please choose one option #command                 !
!                                                                 !
+=================================================================+
```

dBASE II code:

```
@  1, 5 SAY "+=================================================================+"
@  2, 5 SAY "!                                                                 !"
@  3, 5 SAY "!                    FILE   MAINTENANCE   MENU                    !"
@  4, 5 SAY "+=================================================================+"
@  5, 5 SAY "!                                                                 !"
@  6, 5 SAY "!              1. Find and remove duplicate entries               !"
@  7, 5 SAY "!                                                                 !"
@  8, 5 SAY "!              2. Verify new entries                              !"
@  9, 5 SAY "!                                                                 !"
@ 10, 5 SAY "!              3. Verify entries marked for deletion              !"
@ 11, 5 SAY "!                                                                 !"
@ 12, 5 SAY "!              4. Remove entries marked for deletion              !"
@ 13, 5 SAY "!                                                                 !"
@ 14, 5 SAY "!              5. Enter default values for new entries            !"
@ 15, 5 SAY "!                                                                 !"
@ 16, 5 SAY "!              6. Quit to PIP.COM for file backup                 !"
@ 17, 5 SAY "!                                                                 !"
@ 18, 5 SAY "!              7. Return to main menu                             !"
@ 19, 5 SAY "!                                                                 !"
@ 20, 5 SAY "!              Please choose one option"
@ 20,43 GET command
@ 20,64 SAY "!"
@ 21, 5 SAY "!                                                                 !"
@ 22, 5 SAY "+=================================================================+"
```

REPORT.FMT

Screen image:

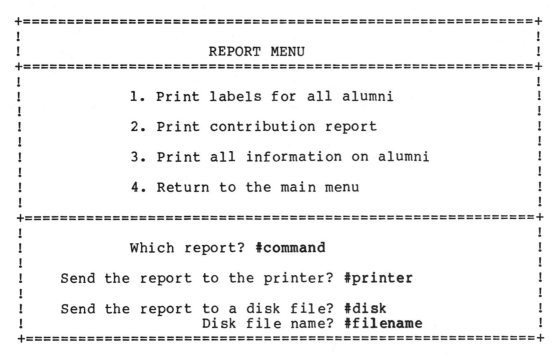

```
+================================================================+
!                                                                !
!                          REPORT MENU                           !
+================================================================+
!                                                                !
!              1. Print labels for all alumni                    !
!                                                                !
!              2. Print contribution report                      !
!                                                                !
!              3. Print all information on alumni                !
!                                                                !
!              4. Return to the main menu                        !
!                                                                !
+================================================================+
!                                                                !
!            Which report? #command                             !
!                                                                !
!      Send the report to the printer? #printer                 !
!                                                                !
!      Send the report to a disk file? #disk                    !
!                     Disk file name? #filename                 !
+================================================================+
```

dBASE II code:

```
@  1, 5 SAY "+================================================================+"
@  2, 5 SAY "!                                                                !"
@  3, 5 SAY "!                          REPORT MENU                           !"
@  4, 5 SAY "+================================================================+"
@  5, 5 SAY "!                                                                !"
@  6, 5 SAY "!              1. Print labels for all alumni                    !"
@  7, 5 SAY "!                                                                !"
@  8, 5 SAY "!              2. Print contribution report                      !"
@  9, 5 SAY "!                                                                !"
@ 10, 5 SAY "!              3. Print all information on alumni                !"
@ 11, 5 SAY "!                                                                !"
@ 12, 5 SAY "!              4. Return to the main menu                        !"
@ 13, 5 SAY "!                                                                !"
@ 14, 5 SAY "+================================================================+"
@ 15, 5 SAY "!                                                                !"
@ 16, 5 SAY "!            Which report?"
@ 16,32 GET command
@ 16,64 SAY "!"
@ 17, 5 SAY "!                                                                !"
```

```
@ 18, 5 SAY "!     Send the report to the printer?"
@ 18,42 GET printer picture "!"
@ 18,64 SAY "!"
@ 19, 5 SAY "!                                                       !
@ 20, 5 SAY "!     Send the report to a disk file?"
@ 20,42 GET disk picture "!"
@ 20,64 SAY "!"
@ 21, 5 SAY "!                     Disk file name?"
@ 21,42 GET filename
@ 21,64 SAY "!"
@ 22, 5 SAY "+===================================================+"
```

<u>SAYDATA.FMT</u>

Screen image:

```
                              @mode
    +================================================================+
    !                                                                !
    !    ID Number @id:no                              @deleted      !
    !                                                                !
    !    First @first               Last @last                       !
    !                                                                !
    !    Address @address                                            !
    !                                                                !
    !    City @city              State @state       Zip @zip          !
    !                                                                !
    !    Phone @phone                                                !
    !                                                                !
    !    Year Graduated @year:grad  Contributions @tot:cont          !
    !                                                                !
    !                                                                !
    +================================================================+
    !  @prompt1                                                      !
    !  @prompt2                                                      !
    !  @prompt3                                                      !
    !                Please choose one option   #command            !
    +================================================================+
```

dBASE II code:

```
@  1,27 SAY mode
@  2, 5 SAY "+=============================================================+"
@  3, 5 SAY "!                                                             !"
@  4, 5 SAY "!    ID Number"
@  4,19 SAY id:no
@  4,51 SAY deleted
@  4,63 SAY "!"
@  5, 5 SAY "!                                                             !"
@  6, 5 SAY "!    First"
@  6,16 SAY first
@  6,33 SAY "Last"
@  6,38 SAY last
@  6,63 SAY "!"
@  7, 5 SAY "!                                                             !"
@  8, 5 SAY "!    Address"
@  8,18 SAY address
@  8,63 SAY "!"
@  9, 5 SAY "!                                                             !"
```

```
@ 10, 5 SAY "!    City"
@ 10,15 SAY city
@ 10,29 SAY "State"
@ 10,35 SAY state
@ 10,45 SAY "Zip"
@ 10,49 SAY zip
@ 10,63 SAY "!"
@ 11, 5 SAY "!
@ 12, 5 SAY "!    Phone"
@ 12,16 SAY phone
@ 12,63 SAY "!"
@ 13, 5 SAY "!
@ 14, 5 SAY "!    Year Graduated"
@ 14,25 SAY year:grad
@ 14,36 SAY "Contributions"
@ 14,49 SAY tot:cont
@ 14,63 SAY "!"
@ 15, 5 SAY "!
@ 16, 5 SAY "!
@ 17, 5 SAY "+==============================================================+
@ 18, 5 SAY "!"
@ 18, 8 SAY prompt1
@ 18,63 SAY "!"
@ 19, 5 SAY "!"
@ 19, 8 SAY prompt2
@ 19,63 SAY "!"
@ 20, 5 SAY "!"
@ 20, 8 SAY prompt3
@ 20,63 SAY "!"
@ 21, 5 SAY "!             Please choose one option"
@ 21,52 GET command picture "!"
@ 21,63 SAY "!"
@ 22, 5 SAY "+==============================================================+
```

TWOSHOW.FMT

Screen image:

```
                              @mode
      +=================================================+
      !    ALUMNI 1                            @deleted1  !
      !                                                   !
      !    ID Number @id:no1                               !
      !    First @first1          Last @last1             !
      !    Address @address1                              !
      !    City @city1          State @state1   Zip @zip1 !
      !    Year Graduated @year:grad1 Contributions @tot:cont1 !
      +-------------------------------------------------+
      !    ALUMNI 2                            @Deleted2  !
      !                                                   !
      !    ID Number @id:no2                               !
      !    First @first2          Last @last2             !
      !    Address @address2                              !
      !    City @city2          State @state2   Zip @zip2 !
      !    Year Graduated @year:grad2 Contributions @tot:cont2 !
      +-------------------------------------------------+
      !    @prompt                                        !
      !    Choose one option #command    Which alumni #alumni  !
      +=================================================+
```

dBASE II code:

```
@  1,27 SAY mode
@  2, 5 SAY "+=================================================+"
@  3, 5 SAY "!    ALUMNI 1"
@  3,51 SAY deleted1
@  3,63 SAY "!"
@  4, 5 SAY "!                                                 !"
@  5, 5 SAY "!    ID Number"
@  5,19 SAY id:no1
@  5,63 SAY "!"
@  6, 5 SAY "!    First"
@  6,15 SAY first1
@  6,32 SAY "Last"
@  6,37 SAY last1
@  6,63 SAY "!"
@  7, 5 SAY "!    Address"
@  7,17 SAY address1
@  7,63 SAY "!"
@  8, 5 SAY "!    City"
```

```
@  8,14 SAY cityl
@  8,30 SAY "State"
@  8,36 SAY statel
@  8,46 SAY "Zip"
@  8,50 SAY zipl
@  8,63 SAY "!"
@  9, 5 SAY "!    Year Graduated"
@  9,24 SAY year:gradl
@  9,36 SAY "Contributions"
@  9,50 SAY tot:contl
@  9,63 SAY "!"
@ 10, 5 SAY "+---------------------------------------------------------+"
@ 11, 5 SAY "!    ALUMNI 2"
@ 11,51 SAY deleted2
@ 11,63 SAY "!"
@ 12, 5 SAY "!                                                         !"
@ 13, 5 SAY "!    ID Number"
@ 13,19 SAY id:no2
@ 13,63 SAY "!"
@ 14, 5 SAY "!    First"
@ 14,15 SAY first2
@ 14,32 SAY "Last"
@ 14,37 SAY last2
@ 14,63 SAY "!"
@ 15, 5 SAY "!    Address"
@ 15,17 SAY address2
@ 15,63 SAY "!"
@ 16, 5 SAY "!    City"
@ 16,14 SAY city2
@ 16,30 SAY "State"
@ 16,36 SAY state2
@ 16,46 SAY "Zip"
@ 16,50 SAY zip2
@ 16,63 SAY "!"
@ 17, 5 SAY "!    Year Graduated"
@ 17,24 SAY year:grad2
@ 17,36 SAY "Contributions"
@ 17,50 SAY tot:cont2
@ 17,63 SAY "!"
@ 18, 5 SAY "+---------------------------------------------------------+"
@ 19, 5 SAY "!"
@ 19, 9 SAY prompt
@ 19,63 SAY "!"
@ 20, 5 SAY "!    Choose one option"
@ 20,27 GET command picture "!"
@ 20,40 SAY "Which alumni"
@ 20,53 GET record
@ 20,63 SAY "!"
@ 21, 5 SAY "+=========================================================+"
```

CHAPTER 7

PROGRAMS FOR A MAILING LIST USING ONE FILE

MAIN.CMD

PSEUDO CODE:

```
    Display the sign on message                      (SIGN-ON)
    Initialize variables and use the file            (INIT)
    Create the main loop of the program
        Check the current record for deletion        (DELCHECK)
        Display the current record, and get the next command
        Do one of the following:
            Add a record                             (ADD)
            Move backward one record
            Delete the current record, or recall it  (DELETE)
            Edit the current record                  (EDIT)
            Move forward one record
            Display a screen of helpful instructions (HELP)
            Present the file maintenance menu        (MAINTAIN)
            Print the current record                 (PRINT)
            Quit to CP/M
            Present the report menu                  (REPORT)
            Search for a record by last name         (SEARCH)
    Loop back and start again
```

FMT FILE USED: SAYDATA.FMT

LOCAL VARIABLES: PROMPT1, PROMPT2, PROMPT3, MODE, and COMMAND

CALLED BY: Started from CP/M with: DBASE MAIN
           Started from dBASE II with: DO MAIN

dBASE II CODE:

```
* main.cmd 12/1/82 abg
* main program of the alumni mailing list system

* display sign on message while initializing the system
DO sign-on

* initialize variables, set up environment, use files, etc.
DO init

* set up the loop
DO WHILE t

    * set up screen and prompts
    SET FORMAT TO saydata
    STORE "A)dd, B)ackward, D)elete/Recall, E)dit" TO prompt1
    STORE "F)orward, H)elp, M)aintenance, P)rint"  TO prompt2
    STORE "Q)uit to operating system, R)eports, S)earch"  TO prompt3
    STORE "Main Menu" TO mode
    STORE " " TO command
```

```
    * find out if the current record is marked for deletion
    DO delcheck

    * show the current record, and find out what to do next
    READ

    * perform selected function
    DO CASE

         CASE command = "A"
         DO add

         CASE command = "B"
         * move backwards one record
         SKIP -1

         CASE command = "D"
         * switch the current record from deleted to recalled
         DO delete

         CASE command = "E"
         DO edit

         CASE command = "F"
         * move forward one record
         SKIP

         CASE command = "H"
         DO help

         CASE command = "M"
         DO maintain

         CASE command = "P"
         DO print

         CASE command = "Q"
         ERASE
         * prevent the dBASE II sign off message
         SET CONSOLE OFF
         QUIT

         CASE command= "R"
         DO report

         CASE command = "S"
         DO search

    ENDCASE

* loop back again
ENDDO
```

<u>SIGN-ON.CMD</u>

PSEUDO CODE:

   Clear the screen
   Display a page of text

CALLED BY: MAIN.CMD

dBASE II CODE:

```
* sign-on.cmd 12/1/82 abg
ERASE
?
?
?
?
?
?
?
?
? "                              Alumni Mailing List System"
?
?
?
?
?
? "                              (C) 1983   SoftwareBanc, Inc."
```

INIT.CMD

PSEUDO CODE:

    Define the working environment of the system
    Create needed memory files
    Use files with proper indices

LOCAL VARIABLES: MID:NO, MFIRST, MLAST, MADDRESS, MCITY, MSTATE,
                   MZIP, MPHONE, MYEAR:GRAD, MTOT:CONT

CALLED BY: MAIN.CMD

dBASE II CODE:

```
* init.cmd 12/1/82 abg
* this program is run once, when main.cmd is first started
* it will initialize the variables, set up the environment, etc.
* place all commands which affect the entire system here

* define environment with set commands
* SET your choice of intensity, bell, confirm, etc
SET TALK OFF
SET INTENSITY OFF

* check for add.mem
* if it isn't there, re-initialize the memory variables
* then save them to a mem file, and clear memory
IF .NOT. FILE( "add.mem" )
    STORE " " TO deleted
    STORE 0 TO mid:no
    STORE "              " TO mfirst
    STORE "              " TO mlast
    STORE "                  " TO maddress
    STORE "            " TO mcity
    STORE "   " TO mstate
    STORE "       " TO mzip
    STORE "              " TO mphone
    STORE "    " TO myear:grad
    STORE 0.00 TO mtot:cont
    SAVE TO add
    RELEASE ALL
ENDIF

* set up file and indices
USE alumni INDEX last, zip, year
```

DELCHECK.CMD

NEW TECHNIQUES:

A record marked for deletion, has an asterisk placed before the first field. By testing for the existence of *, a program may tell if the record is to be deleted. Thus, the instruction IF *, is true for deleted records.

PSEUDO CODE:

    Test the current record for deletion
    Send back the result in the variable called deleted

LOCAL VARIABLE: DELETED

CALLED BY: MAIN.CMD, DUPREM.CMD, VERIFDEL.CMD, VERIFNEW.CMD

dBASE II CODE:

```
* delcheck.cmd 12/1/82 abg
* if the current record is marked for deletion
* then store message to variable for display
* if not, make deleted equal to blank
IF *
    STORE "Deleted" TO deleted
ELSE
    STORE " " TO deleted
ENDIF
```

ADD.CMD

NEW TECHNIQUES:

When using the READ command to enter data into a file, it is best to create a temporary set of variables for use with the FMT file. The data is first READ into these variables, and then placed into a new record, created with the APPEND BLANK command. This will allow editing and validation of the data before it reaches the data file.

The empty variables were created by INIT.CMD, and stored in ADD.MEM.

PSEUDO CODE:

```
    Set up screen for adding records
    Set up a loop to continue until the user is done
        Get a new set of memory variables for data entry
        Display the screen and get the new data
        If an ID number or last name was entered
            Add an empty record to the data file
            Place the entered data into the record
            Mark the record as being newly entered
        If no ID number or last name was entered
            Set up the loop to exit next time around
    Loop back again
    Clear all the local variables from memory
    Put memory back to original state
```

FMT FILE USED: GETDATA.FMT

LOCAL VARIABLES: DELETED,   MID:NO,   MFIRST,   MLAST,   MADDRESS,
                   MCITY,   MSTATE,   MZIP,   MPHONE,   MYEAR:GRAD,
                   MTOT:CONT

                   MODE, PROMPT1, PROMPT2, PROMPT3, MORE

CALLED BY: MAIN.CMD

dBASE II CODE:

```
* add.cmd 12/1/82 abg
* this program will add records to the current file
* the records will be marked as new
* for later verification and merging

* set up screen for data entry
SET FORMAT TO getdata

* loop until finished adding records
STORE t TO more
DO WHILE more
```

```
    * get a new set of memory variables for data entry
    RESTORE from add
    STORE "Add new name and address" TO mode
    STORE "Enter as many names as you want." TO promptl
    STORE "When done, enter blanks for ID, and Last" TO prompt2
    STORE " " TO prompt3
    STORE t TO more

    * let user enter data
    READ

    * place any editing routines here
    * for instance you can make sure a zip code was entered

    * if an ID number or last name was entered
    * add a new record with the entered data
    IF mid:no <> 0 .OR. mlast <>  " "

        * add a new record to the file
        APPEND BLANK

        * fill in the new data
        REPLACE id:no WITH mid:no, first WITH mfirst, last WITH mlast
        REPLACE address WITH maddress, city WITH mcity
        REPLACE state WITH mstate, zip WITH mzip, phone WITH mphone
        REPLACE year:grad WITH myear:grad, tot:cont WITH mtot:cont

        * mark the record as new
        REPLACE new WITH t

    ELSE
        * there are no more records to add
        * set up  the loop to finish
        STORE f TO more

    ENDIF

* loop back again
ENDDO

* release local variables
RELEASE ALL

* restore original variables
STORE "A" TO command
```

DELETE.CMD

PSEUDO CODE:

>   Test the current record for deletion
>   If it has been deleted, then recall it
>   Otherwise delete it

CALLED BY: MAIN.CMD, DUPREM.CMD, VERIFDEL.CMD, VERIFNEW.CMD

dBASE II CODE:

```
* delete.cmd 12/1/82 abg

IF *
    RECALL
ELSE
    DELETE
ENDIF
```

EDIT.CMD

NEW TECHNIQUES:

     Editing a record's data with the READ command is similar to adding new data, in that the current data should be STOREd to temporary variables. The data may then be displayed and changed with the GET command. Once the new data is entered, the program may do the necessary editing and error checking before REPLACEing the data into the record.

     This technique is not required. An FMT file may be used with the actual field variables, but no validation will be possible.

PSEUDO CODE:

    Store the current record's data into temporary variables
    Set up the screen for editing the data
    Let the user edit the data
    Perform any necessary error checking on the new data
    Place the new data into the current record
    Clear all local variables
    Put memory back to its original condition

FMT FILE USED: GETDATA.FMT

LOCAL VARIABLES: MID-NO, MFIRST, MLAST, MADDRESS, MCITY, MSTATE,
                  MZIP, MPHONE, MYEAR:GRAD, MTOT:CONT

                  MODE, PROMPT1, PROMPT2, PROMPT3

CALLED BY: MAIN.CMD, DUPREM.CMD, VERIFNEW.CMD, VERIFDEL.CMD

dBASE II CODE:

```
* edit.cmd 12/1/82 abg
* this program will edit the current record

* save the current memory variables to disk
SAVE TO temp

* store field variables into mem variables for editing
STORE id:no TO mid:no
STORE first TO mfirst
STORE last TO mlast
STORE address TO maddress
STORE city TO mcity
STORE state TO mstate
STORE zip TO mzip
STORE phone TO mphone
STORE year:grad TO myear:grad
STORE tot:cont TO mtot:cont
```

```
* set up screen and prompt for editing
SET FORMAT TO getdata
STORE "Edit name and address" TO mode
STORE "Enter the new name and address information" TO prompt1
STORE " " TO prompt2
STORE " " TO prompt3

* let user enter data
READ

* place any editing routines here
* for instance you can make sure a zip code was entered

* place the edited data back into the same record
REPLACE id:no WITH mid:no, first WITH mfirst
REPLACE last WITH mlast, address WITH maddress
REPLACE city WITH mcity, state WITH mstate
REPLACE zip WITH mzip, phone WITH mphone
REPLACE year:grad WITH myear:grad, tot:cont WITH mtot:cont

* restore original memory
RESTORE FROM temp
```

HELP.CMD

PSEUDO CODE:

    Clear the screen
    Display a screen full of instructions
    Wait for any key to be pressed
    Return to calling program

CALLED BY: MAIN.CMD

dBASE II CODE:

```
* help.cmd 12/1/82 abg
* display a screen full of instructions

ERASE
?
?
? "             Please contact your supervisor for help!"
?
?
?
?
? "                 Press any key to continue"

SET CONSOLE OFF
WAIT
SET CONSOLE ON
```

PRINT.CMD

NEW TECHNIQUES:

     If PRINT is SET ON, all @ SAY statements will be sent to the printer. If the SAY variables have the same names as field variables, the contents of the current record will be printed. This can be used to print the record on custom forms, such as invoices or purchase orders.

PSEUDO CODE:

    Select the printer to accept all @ SAY commands
    Set up the form with field variables
    Send it to the printer

CALLED BY: MAIN.CMD, DUPREM.CMD, VERIFNEW.CMD, VERIFDEL.CMD

dBASE II CODE:

```
* print.cmd 12/1/82 abg
* this will print the current record on the system printer

* assign printer as destination of @ says
SET FORMAT TO PRINT
SET PRINT ON

* print the current record
@  2, 5 SAY "ID Number"
@  2,17 SAY id:no
@  4, 5 SAY "Name"
@  4,17 SAY first
@  4,32 SAY last
@  6, 5 SAY "Address"
@  6,17 SAY address
@  8, 5 SAY "City"
@  8,17 SAY city
@  8,32 SAY state
@  8,42 SAY zip
@ 10, 5 SAY "Phone"
@ 10,17 SAY phone
@ 12, 5 SAY "Year Graduated"
@ 12,22 SAY year:grad
@ 14, 5 SAY "Contributions"
@ 14,22 SAY tot:cont

* turn the printer off
SET PRINT OFF
SET FORMAT TO SCREEN
```

SEARCH.CMD

NEW TECHNIQUES:

Variables used with the FIND command must be used as macros. A "&" must proceed the variable name.

The FIND command will not consider upper case letters the same as lower case. This means that SMITH will not be found, if Smith is searched for. You could require that last names must be entered in upper case. This is not only ugly, but makes the computer less useful than a pad of paper. To avoid this problem, the last name field was INDEXed as capital letters with the !(variable) function. Before doing a FIND the search key is also converted to upper case.

When a FIND is done, the record pointer is moved to the matching record. If there is no match, the record pointer will be equal to zero. The statement # = 0 is true when the record can not be found.

PSEUDO CODE:

```
    Get the last name to search for
    Convert it to upper case
    Try to find the matching record
    If it wasn't found
        Tell the user
    If it was  found
        It is now the current record
```

LOCAL VARIABLE: NAME

CALLED BY: MAIN.CMD

dBASE II CODE:

```
* search.cmd 12/1/82 abg
* this program will search for a record by last name

* clear the screen and ask for the last name
ERASE

?
?
?
?
?
ACCEPT "Please enter the last name to search for" TO name
```

```
* convert name to upper case for searching
STORE !(name) TO name

* look for the matching record
FIND &name

* if it isn't in the file
IF # = 0

    * clear the screen and say that name can't be found
    ERASE
    ?
    ?
    ?
    ?
    ?
    ? name, " is not in the file"
    ? "Press any key to return to the main menu"

    SET CONSOLE OFF
    WAIT
    SET CONSOLE ON

ENDIF

* if the name was found, the record pointer is pointing to it

* release the local variable
RELEASE name
```

MAINTAIN.CMD

PSEUDO CODE:

```
    Set up loop to repeat until the user is done
        Set up menu screen for file maintenance functions
        Perform one of the following:
            Check for duplicates                    (DUPCHECK)
            Verify new entries                      (VERIFNEW)
            Verify records marked for deletion      (VERIFDEL)
            Remove records marked for deletion      (PURGE)
            Add default values for adding records   (DEFAULTS)
            Backup the data files                   (BACKUP)
            Leave this program
    Loop back again
    Clear all local variables
    Put memory back the way it was
```

FMT FILE USED: MAINTAIN.FMT

LOCAL VARIABLE: MORE

CALLED BY: MAIN.CMD

dBASE II CODE:

```
* maintain.cmd 12/1/82 abg
* file maintenance menu

* set up loop
STORE t TO more
DO WHILE more

    * set up screen
    SET FORMAT TO maintain

    * find out what to do next
    STORE " " TO command
    READ

    * perform desired function
    DO CASE

        CASE command = "1"
        * check for duplicates
        DO dupcheck

        CASE command = "2"
        * verify new records
        DO verifnew
```

```
        CASE command = "3"
        * verify deleted records
        DO verifdel

        CASE command = "4"
        * remove records marked for deletion
        DO purge

        CASE command = "5"
        * add new data entry default values
        DO defaults

        CASE command = "6"
        * back up the disk
        DO backup

        CASE command = "7"
        * set up the loop to exit
        STORE f TO more

     ENDCASE

* loop back again
ENDDO

* release local variable
RELEASE more

* restore original data
STORE "M" TO command
```

DUPCHECK.CMD

NEW TECHNIQUES:

To find duplicates for a particular field, INDEX the file on that field, and LIST the entire file. Records which match on the INDEXed field will appear together.

The alumni file should be checked for duplicates on last name. Since it is INDEXed on that field, duplicate entries will be placed next to each other. The program will "walk" through the file in INDEX order, comparing each record against the next.

If the current record is the last in the file, the record pointer will not move on a SKIP. The program must check for EOF when SKIPping, to avoid reading the same record twice, and mistaking it for a duplicate of itself.

PSEUDO CODE:

```
Save the current memory to a MEM file
Start at the first record
Loop until the user is done or end of file is reached
    Display a message while searching is being done
    Save the current record's last name for comparison
    Move to  the next record
    If the new last name is equal to the old last name  and
    end of file has not been reached
        Process the two matching records          (DUPREM)
Loop back and repeat the process with the new current record
Bring back the original memory
```

LOCAL VARIABLES: MORE, OLDLAST

CALLED BY: MAINTAIN.CMD

dBASE II CODE:

```
* dupcheck.cmd 12/1/82 abg
* check for duplicate records based on last name

* since this program will use so many new variables
* save the ones we have now, and restore them when done
SAVE TO temp

* start at the beginning of the file
GOTO TOP

* set up loop to repeat until the whole file has been processed
* or the user decides to quit
STORE t TO more
DO WHILE more .AND. (.NOT. EOF)
```

```
* display something for the user to read
* while the program is searching for duplicates
ERASE
?
?
?
?
?
? "                        Searching for duplicate records"

* save the current last name, in upper case, for comparison
STORE !(last) TO oldlast

* move to the next record to compare
SKIP

* if a match is found and eof has not been reached
* let user look at both, and decide what to do
IF oldlast = !(last) .AND. (.NOT. EOF)
    DO duprem
ENDIF
```

```
* loop back and test again
ENDDO

* restore the original memory
RESTORE FROM temp
```

<u>DUPREM.CMD</u>

PSEUDO CODE:

```
    Move back to the first of the duplicates
    Save its data for display
    Check to see if it has been marked for deletion    (DELCHECK)

    Move forward to the second of the duplicates
    Save its data for display
    Check to see if it has been marked for deletion    (DELCHECK)

    Process the two duplicates until the user is finished
        Set up a screen to display them
        Display both duplicates and find out what to do next
        If the first record is to be processed
            Move back to the first duplicate
        Perform one of the following functions
            Look for more duplicates
            Delete or recall the current record     (DELETE)
            Edit the current record                 (EDIT)
            Print the current record                (PRINT)
            Stop looking for duplicates
        If it was necessary to process the first duplicate
            Move  the record pointer back to the second
    Loop back and process the duplicates again

    If more duplicates are to be found
        Send a message back to DUPCHECK
```

FMT FILE USED: TWOSHOW.FMT

LOCAL VARIABLES: ID:NO1, FIRST1, LAST1, ADDRESS1, CITY1, STATE1,
                   ZIP1, PHONE1, YEAR:GRAD1, TOT:CONT1, DELETED1

                   ID:NO2, FIRST2, LAST2, ADDRESS2, CITY2, STATE2,
                   ZIP2, PHONE2, YEAR:GRAD2, TOT:CONT2, DELETED2

                   PROMPT, MODE, COMMAND, RECORD, MORE

CALLED BY: DUPCHECK.CMD

dBASE II CODE:

```
* duprem.cmd 12/1/82 abg
* this will allow the user to process duplicate records

* get the first duplicate's data to display
SKIP -1

* set up the loop
STORE t TO more
DO WHILE more
    STORE id:no TO id:nol
    STORE first TO firstl
```

```
STORE last TO last1
STORE address TO address1
STORE city TO city1
STORE state TO state1
STORE zip TO zip1
STORE phone TO phone1
STORE year:grad TO year:grad1
STORE tot:cont TO tot:cont1

* find out if this record is marked for deletion
DO delcheck
STORE deleted TO deleted1

* return to the second duplicate record and get its data
SKIP
STORE id:no TO id:no2
STORE first TO first2
STORE last TO last2
STORE address TO address2
STORE city TO city2
STORE state TO state2
STORE zip TO zip2
STORE phone TO phone2
STORE year:grad TO year:grad2
STORE tot:cont TO tot:cont2

* find out if this record is marked for deletion
DO delcheck
STORE deleted TO deleted2

* set up the screen format and variables
SET FORMAT TO twoshow
STORE "C)ontinue, D)elete/Recall, E)dit, P)rint, Q)uit" TO prompt
STORE "Remove Duplicate Records" TO mode
STORE " " TO command
STORE " " TO record

* show both records and find out what to do next
READ

* move to the record to be processed
IF record = "1"
    SKIP -1
ENDIF

* process the record
DO CASE
```

```
            CASE command = "C" .OR. command = "Q"
            * set up the loop to exit
            STORE f TO more

            CASE command = "D"
            DO delete

            CASE command = "E"
            DO delcheck
            DO edit

            CASE command = "P"
            DO print

      ENDCASE

      * move back to correct record
      IF record <> "1"
            SKIP -1
      ENDIF

* loop back again
ENDDO

* if more duplicates are to be found
* set up the loop to continue in DUPCHECK
IF command = "C"
    STORE t TO more
ENDIF
```

VERIFNEW.CMD

NEW TECHNIQUES:

   The LOCATE FOR command is similar to the FIND command, in that it will move the record pointer to the record that matches a specified variable. More than one field may be searched for, and the search fields need not be indexed. The next matching record is found with the CONTINUE command. When no more matching records are found, EOF is made true. LOCATE always starts at the TOP of the file.

PSEUDO CODE:

```
   Start looking for the first new record
   Loop until the user is done or end of file has been reached
        Set up the screen to display the new record
        Check the current record for deletion        (DELCHECK)
        Display it and find out what to do next
        Do one of the following
             Accept the record as permanent
             Delete or recall the current record      (DELETE)
             Edit the current record                  (EDIT)
             Print the current record                 (PRINT)
             Stop looking for new records
             Continue looking for new records
   Loop back again
   Clear local variables
   Put memory back to its original state
```

FMT FILE USED: SAYDATA.FMT

LOCAL VARIABLES: MORE, MODE, PROMPT1, PROMPT2, PROMPT3, COMMAND

CALLED BY: MAINTAIN.CMD

dBASE II CODE:

```
* verifnew.cmd 12/1/82 abg
* verify new records and merge into file

* start looking for new records
LOCATE FOR new

* set up loop
STORE t TO more
DO WHILE more .AND. (.NOT. EOF)

   * set up screen and prompts
   SET FORMAT TO saydata
   STORE "Verify new records" TO mode
```

```
STORE "A)ccept, C)ontinue, D)elete/Recall" TO prompt1
STORE "E)dit, P)rint, Q)uit" TO prompt2
STORE " " TO prompt3
STORE " " TO command

* check to see if the current record is marked for deletion
DO delcheck

* show current record on the screen, ask for input
READ

* process the record
DO CASE

     CASE command = "A"
     * remove mark of a new record
     REPLACE new WITH f

     CASE command = "D"
     DO delete

     CASE command = "E"
     DO edit

     CASE command = "P"
     DO print

     CASE command = "Q"
     *set up loop to exit
     STORE f TO more

     CASE command = "C"
     continue

   ENDCASE

* loop back again
ENDDO

* release local variables
RELEASE mode, prompt1, prompt2, prompt3

* put memory back to its original state
STORE t TO more
STORE "2" TO command
```

VERIFDEL.CMD

PSEUDO CODE:

This program performs the same functions on records which have been marked for deletion, that VERIFNEW performs on new records.

FMT FILE USED: SAYDATA.FMT

LOCAL VARIABLES: MORE, MODE, PROMPT1, PROMPT2, PROMPT3, COMMAND

CALLED BY: MAINTAIN.CMD

dBASE II CODE:

```
* verifdel.cmd 12/1/82 abg
* verify records which have been marked for deletion

* start looking for deleted records
LOCATE FOR *

* set up the loop
STORE t TO more
DO WHILE more .AND. (.NOT. EOF)

    * set up screen
    SET FORMAT TO saydata
    STORE "Verify deleted records" TO mode
    STORE "C)ontinue, E)dit, D)elete/recall, P)rint, Q)uit" TO prompt1
    STORE " " TO prompt2
    STORE " " TO prompt3
    STORE " " TO command

    * check to see if current record is marked for deletion
    DO delcheck

    * show it on the screen
    READ

    * find out what to do next
    DO CASE

        CASE command = "D"
        DO delete

        CASE command = "E"
        DO edit

        CASE command = "P"
         DO print
```

```
          CASE command = "Q"
          STORE f TO more

          CASE command = "C"
          CONTINUE

     ENDCASE

ENDDO

* release local memory variables
RELEASE mode, prompt1, prompt2, prompt3

* put memory back the way it was
STORE t TO more
STORE "3" TO command
```

<u>PURGE.CMD</u>

PSEUDO CODE:

    Clear the screen
    Make sure the user wants to remove the marked records
    If they do want this
        Put up a message to read while removing the records
        Remove records which have been marked for deletion

LOCAL VARIABLE: NEXT

CALLED BY: MAINTAIN.CMD

dBASE II CODE:

```
* purge.cmd 12/1/82 abg
* remove records from the file
* which have been marked for deletion

* scare the user to make sure they want to remove the records
ERASE
?
?
? "***********   WARNING!  ********   WARNING!  ***************"
?
? "This will PERMANENTLY remove any deleted records."
?
? "Type Y to continue, any other key to cancel this operation"

SET CONSOLE OFF
WAIT TO next
SET CONSOLE ON

* if they do want to pack the file
IF !(next) = "Y"

    * give the user something to read while the file is packed
    ERASE
    ?
    ?
    ?
    ? "Records which have been marked for deletion"
    ? "are being removed from the file"

    * pack the file to remove deleted records
    PACK

ENDIF

* release local variables
RELEASE next
```

DEFAULTS.CMD

NEW TECHNIQUES:

Variables are displayed with the @ SAY command, and modified with the @ GET. Default values for data entry may be produced, by storing data into the memory variables used by ADD.CMD for GETDATA.FMT. When a record is added, the default values are accepted when return is typed, or new values are entered to replace the defaults.

PSEUDO CODE:

     Put the current memory variables in temporary storage
     Get the variables used by ADD.CMD
     Set up the screen to enter the new values
     Let the user edit the existing defaults
     Save these new defaults to ADD.MEM
     Get back the original memory variables

FMT FILE USED: GETDATA.FMT

LOCAL VARIABLES: MID:NO, MFIRST, MLAST, MADDRESS, MCITY, MSTATE,
                   MZIP, MPHONE, MYEAR:GRAD, MTOT:CONT
                   PROMPT1, PROMPT2, PROMPT3, MODE

CALLED BY: MAINTAIN.CMD

dBASE II CODE:

```
* defaults.cmd 1/25/82 abg
* this will allow the entry of default variables for ADD.CMD

* get old memory variables for adding records
RESTORE FROM add

* set up screens and prompts
SET FORMAT TO getdata
STORE "Enter data into any field" TO prompt1
STORE "This data will be used when adding records" TO prompt2
STORE " " TO prompt3
STORE "Create new data entry defaults" TO mode

*get the new defaults
READ

* store the new variables
SAVE TO add

* put memory back to its original state
STORE "5" TO command
STORE t TO more
```

BACKUP.CMD

NEW TECHNIQUES:

     The QUIT TO command makes it possible to leave dBASE II, run another program, and return to the dBASE II program. This eliminates the need to train data entry staff in the complexities of CP/M. The QUIT TO command, and this program, will NOT WORK on MS-DOS.

PSEUDO CODE:

     Clear the screen
     Ask if the user wants to backup the data files
     If they do
         Exit to CP/M
         Run PIP.COM
         Return to dBASE II and run MAIN.CMD

LOCAL VARIABLE: NEXT

CALLED BY: MAINTAIN.CMD

dBASE II CODE:

```
* backup.cmd 12/1/82 abg
* make a backup copy of the disk

* clear the screen, and make sure the user wants to do this
ERASE
?
?
?
?
?
? "Type B to backup data, any other key to return to menu"

SET CONSOLE OFF
WAIT TO next
SET CONSOLE ON

* if they do want to backup the files
IF !(next) = "B"
    * exit to cp/m, run pip.com, then restart dbase program
    QUIT TO "pip" , "dbase main"
ENDIF

* release the local variable
RELEASE NEXT
```

REPORT.CMD

NEW TECHNIQUES:

Text that is displayed on the screen may also be saved in a
disk file, identical to a text file created with a word
processor. The SET ALTERNATE TO command creates a file to receive
the text, and SET ALTERNATE ON sends all output to the file.

PSEUDO CODE:

```
    Set up a loop to repeat until the user is done
        Set up the report menu screen and prompts
        Find out what to do next
        If the report goes to the printer
            Turn on the printer
        If the report goes to a disk file and a file name is given
            Send all output to the named file
        Perform one of the following
            Print labels                              (LABEL)
            Print a contribution report               (CONTRIB.FRM)
            Print each alumni's total record          (TOT-REP)
            Leave the report menu
        Turn off the printer
        Stop sending output to the disk file
    Loop back again
    Release local variables
    Return memory to its original state
    Set up the correct indices
```

FMT FILE USED: REPORT.FMT

LOCAL VARIABLES: MORE, PRINTER, DISK, FILENAME, COMMAND

CALLED BY: MAIN.CMD

dBASE II CODE:

```
* report.cmd 12/1/82 abg
* present the report menu

* set up a loop to repeat until the user is done
STORE t TO more
DO WHILE more

    * set up screen and memory variables
    SET FORMAT TO REPORT
    STORE " " TO printer
    STORE " " TO disk
    STORE "              " TO filename
    STORE " " TO command
```

```
    * find out what to do next
    READ

    * set up printer if necessary
    IF printer = "Y"
        SET PRINT ON
    ENDIF

    * send the report to a text file if disk is yes,
    * and a filename has been given
    IF disk = "Y" .AND. filename <> " "
        SET ALTERNATE TO &filename
        SET ALTERNATE ON
    ENDIF

    * clear the screen for the report
    ERASE

    * do the requested report
    DO CASE
        CASE command = "1"
        * use the file in zip code order
        USE alumni INDEX zip
        DO label

        CASE command = "2"
        * use the file in year of graduation order
        USE alumni INDEX year
        REPORT FORM contrib

        CASE command = "3"
        * use the file in last name order
        USE alumni INDEX last
        DO tot-rep

        CASE command = "4"
        STORE f TO more

    ENDCASE
    * turn off the printer and disk file
    * if they were already off this will have no effect
    SET PRINT OFF
    SET ALTERNATE OFF

ENDDO

* release the local variables
RELEASE printer, disk, filename

* restore the original variables
STORE t TO more
STORE "R" TO command

* use the file with all the indices
USE alumni INDEX last,zip,year
```

LABEL.CMD

PSEUDO CODE:

    Set up a loop to print labels for the entire file
        Print labels in the following format
            First Last
            Address
            City, State Zip
        Print 3 blank lines to move to the next label
        Move to the next record
    Loop back again

CALLED BY: REPORT.CMD

dBASE II CODE:

```
* label.cmd 12/1/82 abg
* this program will print mailing labels
* for all alumni

* set up loop to print labels for entire file
DO WHILE .NOT. EOF

    * print one label
    ? TRIM(first), last
    ? address
    ? TRIM(city) -  "," , state, zip
    ?
    ?
    ?

    * move to the next record
    SKIP

* loop back and print the next label
ENDDO
```

CHAPTER 7   PROGRAMS FOR A MAILING LIST USING ONE FILE

<u>CONTRIB.FRM</u>

NEW TECHNIQUES:

    If a report will create subtotals based on the contents of a field, the file should be USEd in order by that INDEX. All records having the same value for the INDEXed field will be placed together.

CALLED BY: REPORT.CMD

. **REPORT FORM CONTRIB**

```
ENTER OPTIONS, M=LEFT MARGIN, L=LINES/PAGE, W=PAGE WIDTH M=0,W=75
PAGE HEADING? (Y/N) Y
ENTER PAGE HEADING: Alumni Contribution Report
DOUBLE SPACE REPORT? (Y/N) N
ARE TOTALS REQUIRED? (Y/N) Y
SUBTOTALS IN REPORT? (Y/N) Y
ENTER SUBTOTALS FIELD: YEAR:GRAD
SUMMARY REPORT ONLY? (Y/N) N
EJECT PAGE AFTER SUBTOTALS? (Y/N) N
ENTER SUBTOTAL HEADING: CONTRIBUTIONS FOR YEAR OF
COL     WIDTH,CONTENTS
001     5,ID:NO
ENTER HEADING:
ARE TOTALS REQUIRED? (Y/N) N
002     10,LAST
ENTER HEADING: NAME
003     10,FIRST
ENTER HEADING:
004     10,CITY
ENTER HEADING: CITY
005     15,TOT:CONT
ENTER HEADING: CONTRIBUTIONS
ARE TOTALS REQUIRED? (Y/N) Y
006     <CR>
```


123

TOT-REP.CMD

NEW TECHNIQUES:

   Printing a report with a program, instead of the REPORT
command,   requires that the programmer calculate the space
available on the page.

Top of page   --

                            Heading of report

                       Data for record number 1

                       Data for record number 2

                       Data for record number 3

                       Data for record number N

Bottom of page   --

Records/page = (page length - heading length) / lines per record

PSEUDO CODE:

   Set up an outer loop so that it repeats until the end of file
      Move to the top of the next page on the printer
      Print the report heading
      Set up inner loop so that it only prints 15 records per
      page and stops if the end of file is reached
         Print the record on three lines
         Increase the count of records printed on this page
         Move to the next record
      Loop back again
   Loop back again

LOCAL VARIABLE: RECORD

CALLED BY: REPORT

dBASE CODE:

```
* tot-rep.cmd 12/1/82 abg
* report to print the entire data record for each alumni

* set up outer loop so that it stops after the last record
DO WHILE .NOT. EOF
```

```
        move to the top of the next page
        EJECT

    * print heading
    ?
    ? "                        Alumni Membership List"
    ? "                        --------------------------"
    ?

    * set up inner loop so that it only prints 15 records per page
    * and stops at the last record
    STORE 0 TO record
    DO WHILE record < 15 .AND. (.NOT. EOF)

        * print the record on four lines
        ? last, first
        ? address, city, state, zip,
        ? "ID NUMBER" ,id:no, "  YEAR GRADUATED" , year:grad, tot:cont
        ?

        * increase the record count
        STORE record + 1 TO record

        * move to the next record
        SKIP

    * loop back and print another record
    ENDDO

* loop back and print a new page
ENDDO

* release the local variable
RELEASE record
```

OUTPUT OF THE THREE REPORTS

LABEL.CMD:

SALLY LADD
14 CONGRESS ST
BOSTON, MA 02126

JOHN JONES
17 SOUTH ST.
WATERTOWN, MA 02156

RAY WATERS
92 ST. BOTOLPH ST.
BOSTON, MA 02234

SAM SMITH
38 BOYLSTON ST
CAMBRIDGE, MA 02235

CONTRIB.FRM:

PAGE NO. 00001

Alumni Contribution Report

ID	NAME		CITY	CONTRIBUTIONS
* CONTRIBUTIONS FOR YEAR OF		68		
1 JONES	JOHN		WATERTOWN	100.00
** SUBTOTAL **				
				100.00
* CONTRIBUTIONS FOR YEAR OF		69		
4 WATERS	RAY		BOSTON	0.00
** SUBTOTAL **				
				0.00
* CONTRIBUTIONS FOR YEAR OF		80		
3 SMITH	SAM		CAMBRIDGE	30.00
2 LADD	SALLY		BOSTON	300.00
** SUBTOTAL **				
				330.00
** TOTAL **				430.00

TOT-REP.CMD:

```
                   Alumni Membership List
                   ----------------------------

JONES              JOHN
17 SOUTH ST.              WATERTOWN   MA 02156
ID NUMBER        1    YEAR GRADUATED  68         100.00


LADD               SALLY
14 CONGRESS ST.           BOSTON      MA 02126
ID NUMBER        2    YEAR GRADUATED  80         300.00


SMITH              SAM
38 BOYLSTON ST.           CAMBRIDGE   MA 02255
ID NUMBER        3    YEAR GRADUATED  80          30.00


WATERS             RAY
92 ST. BOTOLPH ST.        BOSTON      MA 02234
ID NUMBER        4    YEAR GRADUATED  69           0.00
```

CHAPTER 8

LINKING ANOTHER FILE TO ALUMNI.DBF

Our mailing system is now working, and performs the functions specified in the original design. The next step is to add the ability to track individual contributions. The present files contain the total contribution figures for each alumni, but the clerical staff at Story Book University needs more detailed records. They want to record each individual contribution, and cross reference it with the contributing alumni's records.

The simple solution would be to add more fields to ALUMNI.DBF to hold this data. Three fields are needed for each contribution: date, amount, and comments. Unfortunately, there is no way of predicting the number of contributions made by each alumni. Some may have contributed ten times, while others have never given a dime.

If we reserve room in each record for the maximum number of contributions, we will be wasting a great deal of space. Also, each record may can contain thirty two fields. With eleven already in use there is only room for seven sets of contributions. There must be a better way.

This type of problem is solved in dBASE II by storing the individual contribution data in a separate data file, and linking it to the first file. The new file will be called CONTRIB.DBF, and will contain one record for each contribution. This prevents wasted space in the master alumni file, and also allows for the more generous alumni.

Once this new file has been CREATEd, one can perform the necessary cross referencing to the alumni file. Each alumni has been assigned a unique ID number. If each contribution is stored with the contributor's ID number, a program may easily be written to link the two files together.

CREATEing CONTRIB.DBF

The new fields should first be added to the data dictionary for the mailing list system.

Name	Type	Size	Description
Id Number	N	5	This will be used to link each record to the matching alumni in ALUMNI.DBF.
Date	C	8	This will be stored in the
Amount	N	10	
Comments	C	30	This will hold the name of the new wing to be built with the money.

To test the techniques of linking two files, let's CREATE the file and enter some sample data. To be consistent with ALUMNI.DBF, the totals for the sample contributions in CONTRIB.DBF will be equal to the total contributions already entered for each alumni.

. CREATE CONTRIB

ENTER RECORD STRUCTURE AS FOLLOWS:
```
  FIELD    NAME,TYPE,WIDTH,DECIMAL PLACES
  001      ID:NO,N,5
  002      DATE,C,8
  003      AMOUNT,N,10
  004      COMMENT,C,30
  005      <CR>
```

INPUT DATA NOW? **N**

. USE CONTRIB
. APPEND

RECORD 00001
```
ID:NO       : 1
DATE        : 2/3/70
AMOUNT      : 30
COMMENT     :
```

RECORD 00002
```
ID:NO       : 1
DATE        : 3/4/75
AMOUNT      : 70
COMMENT     :
```

RECORD 00003
```
ID:NO       : 2
DATE        : 6/10/81
AMOUNT      : 150
COMMENT     :
```

RECORD 00004
```
ID:NO       : 2
DATE        : 10/10/81
AMOUNT      : 150
COMMENT     :
```

RECORD 00005

ID:NO   : 3
DATE   : 7/5/81
AMOUNT   : 30
COMMENT   :

RECORD 00006

ID:NO   : <CR>

. INDEX ON ID:NO TO CID

00005 RECORDS INDEXED

    Since CONTRIB.DBF will be linked to ALUMNI.DBF on the ID
number, it is a good idea to use the same field name in each
file. It is also necessary to INDEX this new file on the ID
number. This will allow rapid access to all matching
contributions.

    The name for the index field shows that it is based on the
ID number and is for the contribution file.

Linking ALUMNI.DBF with CONTRIB.DBF

    ALUMNI.DBF is USEd in the PRIMARY area of memory and
CONTRIB.DBF is USEd with the ID number index in the SECONDARY
area. When an alumni is selected for cross referencing, the ID
number is used as a key to find the matching records in
CONTRIB.DBF. An example should make this clear.

. USE ALUMNI

. SELECT SECONDARY

. USE CONTRIB INDEX CID

. SELECT PRIMARY

. DISPLAY LAST,ID:NO

00001 JONES   1

. SELECT SECONDARY

. FIND 1

. DISPLAY

```
00001         1 2/3/70            30.00
```

   This is all it takes to find the first matching record.
Since CONTRIB.DBF is in index order by ID number, all of the
records with the same ID number will be placed together. We
simply SKIP to find the next match. When the ID number changes,
we know that all of the matching contributions have been found.

. SKIP

RECORD: 00002

. DISPLAY

```
00002         1 3/4/75            70.00
```

. SKIP

RECORD: 00003

. DISPLAY

```
00003         2 6/10/81          150.00
```

   There is one more technique to be learned before writing a
program to link files. In our example, we looked at the ID number
of the alumni and used that number with the FIND command. Our
program will store the ID number to a variable. Variables used
with the FIND command must be used as macros, and macros must be
of character type. The ID number is of numeric type, so it must
be converted to character with the STR function. This function
takes the variable name and length as arguments, and returns the
same variable as characters. It sounds complicated, but it is
only one extra step in a program.

Pseudo code for LINK.CMD

Use ALUMNI.DBF with the last name index in the primary area
Use CONTRIB.DBF with the ID number index in the secondary area
Ask the name of the alumni to search for
Find that alumni's record
Do one of the following:
     If the alumni can't be found
          Tell the user
     If the alumni has never contributed
          Tell the user
     Find the first matching contribution
          Show all other contributions with matching ID numbers

<u>dBASE</u> <u>II</u> <u>code</u>

```
-----------------------------------------------------------------
.  MODIFY COMMAND LINK

* link.cmd   12/1/82 abg

* sample program to link files on a field in common
SET TALK OFF

* use the two files
USE ALUMNI INDEX LAST
SELECT SECONDARY
USE CONTRIB INDEX CID
SELECT PRIMARY

* find out the name of the desired alumni
ACCEPT "Please enter the last name of the alumni to find" TO NAME

* convert the name to upper case and find the right record
STORE !(NAME) TO NAME
FIND &NAME

* perform one of the following
DO CASE

     case # = 0
     * alumni can't be found
     ? NAME, "is not in the file"
     ? "Press return to continue"
     SET CONSOLE OFF
     WAIT
     SET CONSOLE ON

     CASE TOT:CONT = 0
     * this alumni has never contributed
     ? "Don't waste your time with the cheapskate"

     OTHERWISE
     * convert ID number to character type
     STORE STR(ID:NO,5) TO key

     * move to the contribution file
     SELECT SECONDARY

     * find the first matching record
     find &key

     * print a heading
     ? "The contributions for", name, "are:"
```

134

```
      * show each contribution until the end of the file
      * or a new ID number is reached
      DO WHILE .NOT. EOF .AND. STR(id:no,5) = key


            * show a contribution record
            ? date, amount, comment

            * move to the next record
            SKIP

      * loop back
      ENDDO

ENDCASE

* release local variables
RELEASE   key, name

* move back to the primary area of memory
SELECT PRIMARY
```

. **DO LINK**

Please enter the last name of the alumni to find:**Jones**

The contributions for JONES are:
2/3/70   30.00
3/4/75   70.00

. **DO LINK**

Please enter the last name of the alumni to find:**Waters**

Don't waste your time with the cheapskate

. **DO LINK**

Please enter the last name of the alumni to find:**Symes**

SYMES is not in the file
Press return to continue

Designing a complete contribution system

If programs are written in a modular fashion, as ours were, it is never hard to link in new systems and files. With the techniques presented in this book you should now be able to write a set of programs which perform the following functions:

Add a contribution   (CADD)

Edit a contribution   (CEDIT)

Delete a contribution   (CDELETE)

Print a report listing all contributions for all alumni
                                            (CTOT-REP)

Show all contributions of a given alumni (CSHOW)

Return to the main menu

CHAPTER 9

INTERFACING dBASE II WITH SUPERCALC AND WORDSTAR

The true power of dBASE II becomes apparent when it is used with other types of programs. The ideal computer system would provide the user with a complete set of general purpose programs, which would all work with the same data. A data base program could collect the figures, which would be analyzed by a financial modeling program, then formatted and printed by a word processor. Of course, the data would only be typed into the computer once.

The pieces of this system exist in dBASE II, SuperCalc, and WordStar, and the necessary interaction is almost here. Data can be printed to a file from dBASE II and SuperCalc for use with a word processor such as WordStar, and figures from SuperCalc can be transferred to dBASE II. The missing link is the ability to enter data into SuperCalc from other programs without re-typing it, and this should be accomplished in the near future.

The major hurdle in creating this ideal interactive system is getting the publishers of each of these programs to cooperate. For   political and economic reasons,   these companies are reluctant to publicize techniques that would encourage users of their programs to purchase products produced by others. The information is available in the manuals, but it is not spelled out for the novice.

This chapter will demonstrate these techniques with a sample budget keeping application.   WordStar will be used in the examples, but any CP/M or MS-DOS word processor will work as well.

From dBASE II to WordStar

Word processors running under the CP/M or MS-DOS operating systems can all read the same type of file, called a text file, which contains only characters that can be printed. If you like acronyms, these text files are also called ASCII files.

To save the output of dBASE II, or a program written in the dBASE II language, a file must first be created to receive the text. To tell dBASE II to start a file called SAMPLE, the instruction SET ALTERNATE TO SAMPLE would be entered. An empty file called SAMPLE.TXT would then be created on the disk. When the command SET ALTERNATE ON is given, all text which appears on the screen will be saved in this file. SET ALTERNATE OFF will stop this process.

This technique will allow you to use all of your word processor's formatting capabilities on a report before it is printed. This book is an example of merging dBASE II output into the body of a report.

From SuperCalc to a text file

Transferring a SuperCalc model to a text file is similar in form, but different commands are required. When a model is ready for printing, instructions are given which define the destination of the output and the portion of the model to be printed. The following commands will send a sample budget created with SuperCalc to a text file.

/Output, Display, Al:E20, Disk, BUDGET1.TXT

```
   |    A    ||    B    ||    C    ||    D    ||    E    |
 1|Sample Monthly Expense Summary -- to be transferred to dBASE II
 2|
 3|Category         Budget      % of Budget Actual
 4|-------------------------------------------------------
 5|Rent             500.00         .30        500.00
 6|Phone            100.00         .06        150.00
 7|Oil              150.00         .09        250.00
 8|Electric          30.00         .02         29.00
 9|Car payments     150.00         .09        150.00
10|Car insurance     40.00         .02         40.00
11|Food             350.00         .21        300.00
12|Entertainment     50.00         .03         20.00
13|Car gas & oil     40.00         .02         45.00
14|Lunches          130.00         .08        167.00
15|Books             20.00         .01         14.00
16|Clothes           50.00         .03          .00
17|Laundry           30.00         .02         33.00
18|              ============= =========== ============
19|                1640.00        1.00       1698.00
20|
```

This set of figures is a comparison of budgeted to actual monthly expenses. This type of analysis is most often done in a spread sheet such as SuperCalc.

If this report is to be studied in greater detail, the formulas for each entry may also be displayed and printed to a file.

/Global, Formula
/Output, Display, Al:E20, Disk, BUDGET2.TXT

```
     |    A    ||    B   ||    C    ||    D   ||    E    |
 1|Sample Monthly Expense Summary -- to be transferred to dBASE II
 2|
 3|Category        Budget       % of Budget Actual
 4|-------------------------------------------------------
 5|Rent            500          B5/B19        500
 6|Phone           100          B6/B19        150
 7|Oil             150          B7/B19        250
 8|Electric         30          B8/B19         29
 9|Car payments    150          B9/B19        150
10|Car insurance    40          B10/B19        40
11|Food            350          B11/B19       300
12|Entertainment    50          B12/B19        20
13|Car gas & oil    40          B13/B19        45
14|Lunches         130          B14/B19       167
15|Books            20          B15/B19        14
16|Clothes          50          B16/B19         0
17|Laundry          30          B17/B19        33
18|             =============  ==========  ============
19|             SUM(B4:B18)  SUM(C4:C18)  SUM(D4:D18)
20|
```

In order to bring these figures into a dBASE II data file,
only the data must be sent to the disk. The borders must be
removed, and the title can't be printed. The range of entries to
be printed must be limited to those which contain actual data.

/Global, Border
/Output, Display, A5:D17, Disk, SCDATA.TXT


```
Rent                500.00       .30      500.00
Phone               100.00       .06      150.00
Oil                 150.00       .09      250.00
Electric             30.00       .02       29.00
Car payments        150.00       .09      150.00
Car insurance        40.00       .02       40.00
Food                350.00       .21      300.00
Entertainment        50.00       .03       20.00
Car gas & oil        40.00       .02       45.00
Lunches             130.00       .08      167.00
Books                20.00       .01       14.00
```

Once these files are on the disk they may be read into a
word processor and incorporated in the text of any report.

Text file to dBASE II

The APPEND FROM command may be used to take data from a text file and place it into a dBASE II DBF file. The data in a DBF file is stored with a header at the front. dBASE II can then tell the name, size, and type of every field. Since the text file does not have a header, dBASE II must be given another means of identifying individual fields.

The simplest method is to use the relative position of the data within the file. Each record should be thought of as a single line of text. Within that line each field is assigned a specific range of characters. The space allocated to each field is specified with the WIDTH command in SuperCalc. Here are the filed widths of SCDATA.TXT.

```
Clothes              50.00        .03        .00
Laundry              30.00        .02      33.00
|    15     |     10     |     10    |     10     |
```

The SuperCalc data has been printed to the file with each column assigned to a specific range of characters. The names for the columns have not been included.

This information may now be used to create a matching DBF file. A field must be defined for each range of characters in the text file. The sizes of the fields must be identical to the SuperCalc column sizes, however any name may be used.

A>DBASE

. CREATE BUDGET

ENTER RECORD STRUCTURE AS FOLLOWS:
  FIELD   NAME,TYPE,WIDTH,DECIMAL PLACES
  001   CATEGORY,C,15
  002   BUDGET,N,10,2
  003   PCNT:BUDG,N,10,2
  004   ACTUAL,N,10,2
  005   <CR>
INPUT DATA NOW? N

The data is brought into the file with the command APPEND FROM SCDATA.TXT. To tell dBASE II that the file does not have a header, but is a normal text file, the SDF clause is added to the instruction. dBASE II will read the first line of SCDATA.TXT and place the first 15 characters into the category field. Each field will be filled in this way, until the entire file has been read.

. USE BUDGET

. APPEND FROM SCDATA.TXT SDF

00013 RECORDS ADDED

. LIST

00001	Rent	500.00	0.30	500.00
00002	Phone	100.00	0.06	150.00
00003	Oil	150.00	0.09	250.00
00004	Electric	30.00	0.02	29.00
00005	Car payments	150.00	0.09	150.00
00006	Car insurance	40.00	0.02	40.00
00007	Food	350.00	0.21	300.00
00008	Entertainment	50.00	0.03	20.00
00009	Car gas & oil	40.00	0.02	45.00
00010	Lunches	130.00	0.08	167.00
00011	Books	20.00	0.01	14.00
00012	Clothes	50.00	0.03	0.00
00013	Laundry	30.00	0.02	33.00

    Once the data is in the DBF file all of the usual commands
apply. The REPORT command may be used to format it in a more
formal way.

. INDEX ON CATEGORY TO CATEGORY

. LIST

00011	Books	20.00	0.01	14.00
00009	Car gas & oil	40.00	0.02	45.00
00006	Car insurance	40.00	0.02	40.00
00005	Car payments	150.00	0.09	150.00
00012	Clothes	50.00	0.03	0.00
00004	Electric	30.00	0.02	29.00
00008	Entertainment	50.00	0.03	20.00
00007	Food	350.00	0.21	300.00
00013	Laundry	30.00	0.02	33.00
00010	Lunches	130.00	0.08	167.00
00003	Oil	150.00	0.09	250.00
00002	Phone	100.00	0.06	150.00
00001	Rent	500.00	0.30	500.00

```
. REPORT FORM BUDGET
ENTER OPTIONS, M=LEFT MARGIN, L=LINES/PAGE, W=PAGE WIDTH
PAGE HEADING? (Y/N) Y
ENTER PAGE HEADING: Budget data obtained from SuperCalc
DOUBLE SPACE REPORT? (Y/N) N
ARE TOTALS REQUIRED? (Y/N) Y
SUBTOTALS IN REPORT? (Y/N) N
COL      WIDTH,CONTENTS
001      15,CATEGORY
ENTER HEADING: CATEGORY
002      10,BUDGET
ENTER HEADING: BUDGET
ARE TOTALS REQUIRED? (Y/N) Y
003      10,PCNT:BUDG
ENTER HEADING: % BUDGET
ARE TOTALS REQUIRED? (Y/N) Y
004      10,ACTUAL
ENTER HEADING: ACTUAL
ARE TOTALS REQUIRED? (Y/N) Y
005      <CR>
```

PAGE NO. 00001

Budget Data Obtained from SuperCalc

CATEGORY	BUDGET	% BUDGET	ACTUAL
Books	20.00	0.01	14.00
Car gas & oil	40.00	0.02	45.00
Car insurance	40.00	0.02	40.00
Car payments	150.00	0.09	150.00
Clothes	50.00	0.03	0.00
Electric	30.00	0.02	29.00
Entertainment	50.00	0.03	20.00
Food	350.00	0.21	300.00
Laundry	30.00	0.02	33.00
Lunches	130.00	0.08	167.00
Oil	150.00	0.09	250.00
Phone	100.00	0.06	150.00
Rent	500.00	0.30	500.00
** TOTAL **			
	1640.00	0.98	1698.00

BIBLIOGRAPHY

CP/M:

Hogan, T., <u>CP/M User Guide</u>, Osborne/McGraw-Hill, 1981

Zaks, R., <u>The CP/M Handbook</u>, Sybex, 1980

DATA BASE APPLICATIONS:

Martin, J., <u>An End-User's Guide To Data Base</u>, Prentice Hall, 1981

Martin, J., <u>Computer Data-Base Organization</u>, Prentice Hall, 1977

Martin, J., <u>Design And Strategy For Distributed Data Processing</u>, Prentice Hall, 1981

DATA BASE THEORY:

Knuth, D. E., <u>Sorting And Searching</u>, Addison-Wesley, 1973

INTRODUCTION TO COMPUTERS:

Osborne, A., <u>Business System Buyer's Guide</u>, Osborne/McGraw Hill, 1981

Walter, R., <u>The Secret Guide To Computers Vols. 1-8</u>, Russ Walter, 1982

Zaks, R., <u>How To Care For Your Computer</u>, Sybex, 1981

PROGRAMMING TECHNIQUES:

Martin, J., <u>Design of Man-Computer Dialogues</u>, Prentice Hall, 1973

Nevison, J. M., <u>The Little Book of Basic Style</u>, Addison-Wesley, 1978

FILES USED IN THE BOOK

TYPE	NAME	PAGES
CMD	ADD	97
	BACKUP	119
	DEFAULTS	118
	DELCHECK	96
	DELETE	99
	DUPCHECK	108
	DUPREM	110
	EDIT	100
	HELP	102
	INIT	95
	LAB-SEL	46
	LABEL	42,122
	LINK	134
	MAIN	92
	MAINTAIN	106
	MENU	49
	PRINT	103
	PURGE	117
	REPORT	120
	SAMPLE	37
	SAMPLE2	42
	SCREEN1	60
	SEARCH	104
	SIGN-ON	94
	TEST	65
	TOT-REP	124
	VERIFDEL	115
	VERIFNEW	113
DBF	ALUMNI	78
	BUDGET	141
	CONTRIB	130
	MAIL	11
	MAILZIP	15
	NEWMAIL	29
	NEWMAIL2	30
	NEWMAIL3	30
	NEWMAIL4	34
	TEST	20
	TEST2	22
FMT	GETDATA	82
	MAINTAIN	84
	REPORT	85
	SAYDATA	87
	TWOSHOW	89
FRM	BUDGET	143
	CONTRIB	123
	MAILIST	18
MEM	ADD	82
	TEST	23

INDEX

INDEX

INDEX

DISK VERSION OF MAILING LIST SYSTEM AVAILABLE!

Learn dBASE II Faster

No Typing Required

The best way to learn any language is to use it. To ease your introduction to dBASE II, the sample mailing list system described in this book is available in disk form.

This disk will help you study a complete dBASE II application. All of the programs described in Chapters 7 and 8 are ready to be put to use immediately. Of course, you can also modify the programs for your own application. Many dBASE II users have made these programs the foundation for much larger systems.

To order your copy of the dBASE II User's Guide Disk, just fill out the order form and mail it along with $29, (this includes postage), to:

        SoftwareBanc
        dBASE II User's Guide Disk
        661 Mass. Ave.
        Arlington, MA.   02174
        (617) 641-1241

Payment may be made by: check, MasterCard, Visa, or money order. Please include your computer type and disk size when ordering.

Registration and Disk Order Form

| | I would like to be notified of new versions of this book, and any future books on dBASE II.

| | I would like to receive information about the dBASE II classes taught by Adam B. Green.

Name   _____   Phone Number

Company   _____   _____

Address   _____

City   _____   State _____   Zip _____

Comments on this edition   _____

_____

_____

_____

_____

****

| | I would like to order the sample mailing list system in disk form.

No. of Disks	Unit Price	Total Price
	$ 29	

Type of computer _____

Size of disk 8"   5 1/4"

Payment is enclosed:
| | Check | | Money order
| | MasterCard | | VISA

Credit card no. _____

Expiration date __/__   Signature _____

Mail To: SoftwareBanc
               dBASE II User's Guide Disk
               661 Mass. Ave.
               Arlington, MA. 02174